T0212775

Human-Computer Interaction Series

HCI is a multidisciplinary field focused on human aspects of the development of computer technology. As computer-based technology becomes increasingly pervasive—not just in developed countries, but worldwide—the need to take a human-centered approach in the design and development of this technology becomes ever more important. For roughly 30 years now, researchers and practitioners in computational and behavioral sciences have worked to identify theory and practice that influences the direction of these technologies, and this diverse work makes up the field of human-computer interaction. Broadly speaking it includes the study of what technology might be able to do for people and how people might interact with the technology. The HCI series publishes books that advance the science and technology of developing systems which are both effective and satisfying for people in a wide variety of contexts. Titles focus on theoretical perspectives (such as formal approaches drawn from a variety of behavioral sciences), practical approaches (such as the techniques for effectively integrating user needs in system development), and social issues (such as the determinants of utility, usability and acceptability).

Titles published within the Human-Computer Interaction Series are included in Thomson Reuters' Book Citation Index, The DBLP Computer Science Bibliography and The HCI Bibliography.

More information about this series at http://www.springer.com/series/6033

Pradipta Biswas

Inclusive Human Machine Interaction for India

A Case Study of Developing Inclusive Applications for the Indian Population

Pradipta Biswas

University of Cambridge Department of Engineering
Cambridge, Cambridgeshire
United Kingdom

 Springer

Pradipta Biswas
University of Cambridge
Department of Engineering
Cambridge
Cambridgeshire
United Kingdom

ISSN 1571-5035
ISBN 978-3-319-35889-5   ISBN 978-3-319-06500-7 (eBook)
DOI 10.1007/978-3-319-06500-7
Springer Cham Heidelberg New York Dordrecht London

Printed on acid-free paper

Springer is part of Springer Science+Business Media (www.springer.com)

Foreword

Having made a mark in providing ICT based-services to significant parts of the developed world, India has begun focusing over the last decade to proliferate usage of ICT in every aspect of life of its citizens. While most of the youngsters readily adapt to the host of electronic devices available today, irrespective of the region and educational background that they come from, this is not true for the elderly population. The aged, in particular, and especially if their educational background is limited, find difficult to master and use different devices readily. Poor-eyesight, stiffness of limbs, inability to move their fingers as rapidly and similar such limits that emerge with age, makes the user-interfaces, available with these new devices, difficult to use.

This book comes in as timely reminder to limits of technologies and human–machine interface, which have been developed without taking into account needs of this section of population. As discussed in the book, "the diversity of language, culture, and geography" in India, makes it particularly important to address this aspect. The study further points out that the solutions do exist; just that sufficient attention has not been paid to them in India. Further, with their technological abilities, India's young IT professionals are in advantageous position to address this problem and make design of inclusive human–machine interface as an integral part of all its development work. If they are able to do that, they would not only address this problem for India but "technologies developed for common people of India will find useful applications in other developed countries."

The book, for the first time, does a systematic study of human–computer interface for the aged population in India in different parts of the country. It has sufficient data for one to begin understanding the problem. In that sense, it will be a useful study for young students and scholars who wish to train themselves in this field or in developing IT solutions for common people of India.

Prof. Ashok Jhunjhunwala

- Professor of the Department of Electrical Engineering, Indian Institute of Technology, Chennai, India
- Director in the Board of SBI, TTML, BEL, Polaris, 3i Infotech, Sasken, Tejas, NRDC, and IDRBT
- Member of Prime Minister's Setup Scientific Advisory Committee

Introduction

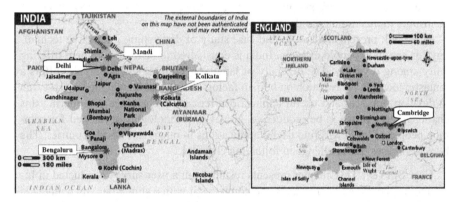

Surveys and trials reported in this book were conducted at Mandi, Delhi, Kolkata and Bangalore in India and Cambridge in UK

Mr. and Mrs. Gonsalvez[1] live in Bangalore. Their son works in a multinational company in US. Mr. Gonsalves has retired from a Telecommunication firm and is still very interested and proud about his son's work and achievement. He is 84, already lost part of vision and hearing, but still reads a lot of magazines and if finds something interesting, he reports it to his son. However, talking to US for long time is pretty costly. So the Gonsalves couple went to a local cyber training school to learn email technology, video conferencing, and Internet browsing. It was a new world for them. Mrs. Gonsalvez also rekindled her old hobby of embroidering by downloading new designs from Internet. But all did not go well. They failed to remember how to use the mouse, how to operate the email client, how to attach photographs, surf Internet, and so on. Presently Mr. Gonsalves does not use computer himself, rather he pastes interesting news clips, their photographs or any other message on a sheet of paper and then takes it to a cyber café. The local computer guy scans it and sends it to his son.

Shrimati (Mrs.) Nilima Devi[1] is 87-year-old and lives in an old-age home at Mandi in Himachal Pradesh. She is well educated in Hindi, still regularly reads

---

[1] The names are not real but the use cases are true.

holy religious books but cannot read English. She has high-powered glasses and also has slight tremor in hand. However, she has no problem in operating her mobile phone, which does not support local language. She cannot SMS, but apart from that, not only can make and receive calls but also plays her favorite songs by browsing through the menu hierarchy and song list.

Rapid advancement of interactive technologies during the past two decades has made access to information easier for us however at the expense of a clear digital divide. There is a generation who grew up with these technologies while there are a lot of people who still find a lot of modern electronic systems counter intuitive and do not find any use of these in their daily life. This digital divide becomes more prominent in developing countries as state-of-the-art interactive systems were not or even are still not affordable to a lot of users. Differences in lifestyle, culture, and prior experience between people of developed and developing countries also often contribute to this digital divide.

This book presents an end-to-end case study of developing interactive technology for common people of India. India is considered to be a subcontinent offering unity among diversity. The diversity of language, culture, and geography offers a fantastic location for research on human factors. However, leveraging this research to develop practical and useful applications remains a challenge. Countering this challenge may prove to be productive, however, technologies developed for common people of India will find useful applications in other developed countries. The book addresses this challenge in following chapters.

- **User Survey:** This chapter presents results from a user survey conducted in India. It focuses on elderly users and compares it with a similar survey conducted in Europe. The chapter concludes by summarizing a few design guidelines.
- **User Model:** This chapter summarizes the Inclusive User Model that can simulate users' interaction patterns and can adapt interfaces for a wide variety of users and applications. The chapter provides detail on the integration of the model to personalize interfaces for a wide range of applications and user trials to evaluate these adapted applications in Indian context.
- **User Interaction:** This chapter presents detail on novel modalities of interaction like eye-gaze and head tracking interfaces. It discusses detail of a target prediction technology that facilitates human machine interaction using these new modalities of interaction. In particular, it proposes a Neural Network based model that can be used to predict pointing target for both physical and situational impairment. The model takes different trajectory profiles like velocity, acceleration, and bearing of movement as input parameters, and based on that, predicts next pointing target. The chapter reports three user studies—one involving users with physical and age-related impairment using a mouse and the other two involve able-bodied users using head and eye-gaze tracking based systems.
- **New Interfaces:** This chapter proposes a set of new user interfaces to facilitate interaction for applications that are used almost every day by computer-literate people. It presents new graphical user interfaces for electronic shopping, banking, traveling applications, and so on. The user interfaces are especially targeted to people who do not know computers well or have age-related physical or cog-

nitive impairment. The chapter also presents a few user trials those involved an eye-gaze tracker to operate these new interfaces.

- **Conclusion:** The last chapter summarizes the overall content of the book and discusses about future research scopes for developing world.
- The **Appendix** contains a sample consent form used in the user trial, a sample of NASA TLX score sheet, and description of a user profile format proposed in the book and published by ITU-T.

Aim of the Book

This book primarily focused on researchers, students, and practitioners of India involved in designing electronic user interfaces and web sites. However, discussions on the user modeling web services, eye-gaze tracking system, and user trials should be useful for all interaction designers. For any interface or interaction designer, covering the huge population of India and its inherent diversity is a tremendous challenge. However, a few minor tweaks in interface can often significantly increase the usability of a whole system. For example, let us consider the use case of booking a train using the website of Indian Railway Catering and Tourism Corporation Limited (IRCTC). Indian railway network was the third biggest in world at the time of writing this book (after USA, China, and Russia) and the IRCTC website has undoubtedly made railway reservation easier. Figure 1 below shows three screenshots in the process of booking a train.

Screen 1

Screen 2

Screen 3

The first screen is a simple LogIn screen. Interestingly, the second screen has the 'Reset' button almost in the same relative position of the 'LogIn' button of the first screen, which increases the chance of accidentally clearing the form. The spacing of the 'FindTrains' and 'Reset' button also contributes to missed selection if the user has tremor in hand or using a small-screen device like a Smartphone or tablet. Finally, the third screen uses small font size, does not offer any explanation of the abbreviations of coach names, (1A, CC etc.) and only the small red script at the top right corner tells how to book a train from the list, which will not only be missed by users with visual impairment but also by non-expert users.

This book starts with a survey highlighting subjective requirements of users. Then it proposes a technology to personalize interfaces which can enhance usability of interfaces like the one discussed above. The book looks forward to new modalities of interaction like eye-gaze and head tracking systems and discusses about their prospect of being incorporated in everyday computing applications. The book also presents details of a lot of user trials and can solely be used as a guideline to design controlled experiments on software applications. The user trials also highlight the gap between designers and users viewpoints and the results can be extrapolated for any application.

University of Cambridge   Pradipta Biswas
Department of Engineering
Cambridge
Cambridgeshire
United Kingdom

Unique Features of this Book

- **HCI book for India:** A first attempt to address challenges in developing state-of-the-art interactive technology for Indian population.
- **Bridging digital divide involving state-of-the-art technology:** Investigation on using latest interactive devices like eye-gaze tracker or Brain computer interfaces for common users including people with age related or physical impairment for everyday computing like online shopping, banking, and so on.
- **An inclusive end-to-end case study:** A report starting from user survey to user validation for developing personalized applications covers the whole life cycle of developing interactive systems.

Acknowledgement

At first, I would like to thank all participants of the survey and trials described in this book. Without their active help and support, this book would not have been possible. I am grateful to all colleagues of IUATC project, especially, the PIs Prof. Gerrard Parr, Prof. Nader Azarmi, and Prof. Ashok Jhunjhunwala. The project was funded by UK EPSRC, BT, and Department of Science and Technology (DST) of Government of India. In particular, special mention is deserved by Dr. Patrick Langdon of University of Cambridge, Ms. Jayalakshmi Umadikar of RTBI, Indian Institute of Technology, Madras, Dr. Sanat Sarangi and Prof. Subrat Kar of Indian Institute of Technology, Delhi, and Prof. Arti Kashyap of Indian Institute of Technology, Mandi, for their active support in conducting the user trials.

University of Cambridge   Pradipta Biswas
Department of Engineering
Cambridge
Cambridgeshire
United Kingdom

Contents

Chapter 1
User Survey

People were excited and supportive to our user survey at Mandi

1.1 Introduction

Human–computer interaction (HCI) is about knowing the user, which becomes more important while we consider users with different range of abilities in a developing country. This chapter reports a survey to estimate Indian elderly and disabled users' perceptual, cognitive, and motor capabilities, and also their experience and attitude towards technology. We have initially identified functional parameters [3, 4, 6] that can affect users' interaction with electronic devices and combined both objective metrics on functional parameters and subjective attitude towards technology. Previous surveys, either concentrated on ergonomics or demographic details of European

P. Biswas, *Inclusive Human Machine Interaction for India,*
Human–Computer Interaction Series, DOI 10.1007/978-3-319-06500-7_1,
© Springer International Publishing Switzerland 2014

people [13] or focused on a particular device like digital TV or mobile phones [10, 11]. There is not much reported work on capabilities and attitude towards technology of older Indian population, especially from an HCI point of view.

It is well known that there are social, economical and cultural differences between people living in different countries in Europe [8, 14, 15]. So we used data from a previous survey [9] to compare the results on Indian population with their European counterparts.

Our study found that there is a significant effect of age on hand strength of elderly users limiting their use of standard computer peripherals. It is also found that European elderly users tend to score higher in cognitive tests than their Indian counterparts and for the Indian population; there is a significant correlation between education level and cognitive abilities. We also found that elderly people acknowledge the need of using new technologies, though they prefer to use TV and mobile phones than computers. The chapter also points out the implication of the findings for designers in Sect. 4.

1.2   Survey

Our survey estimates users' perceptual, cognitive, and motor capabilities and also their experience and attitude towards technology. The following subsections discuss details on the survey.

1.2.1   Place of Survey

The survey was conducted at Mandi, Himachal Pradesh; Kolkata, West Bengal; and Bangalore, Karnataka. The survey was conducted at old-age homes and participants volunteered for the study. We also collected data from nine young people with physical impairment at an orthopedic hospital in Kolkata.

For comparative analysis with European population, we used results from a previous survey conducted in the UK, Spain and Germany.

1.2.2   Participants

We collected data from 33 users. Figure 1.1 below shows an age histogram where 10 users were female and 23 were male. Nine users were younger but had physical impairment as listed in Table 1.1 below.

We have also used results from a previous survey conducted on approximately 30 people at Spain, UK and Germany. Details of that survey and demographic detail on users can be found in a separate report [9]. We used that data to compare performances and attitudes of Indian population to their European counterpart.

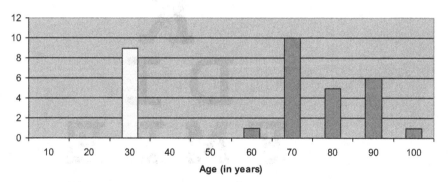

Fig. 1.1. Age histogram of Indian sample

Table 1.1 Description of younger users

Age	Sex	Disability
26	F	Polio
30	F	Polio
25	F	Polio
26	M	Polio
27	F	Birth defect
26	M	Birth defect
27	M	Lost one hand in accident
28	M	Lost one hand in accident

1.2.3 Functional Parameters Measurement

We measured objective parameters about perceptual, cognitive and motor abilities of users using standard test batteries. We have measured the following parameters based on our previous studies which identified them as relevant for interaction with electronic devices.

Minimum Font Size (FS) We measured it using a Snellen chart (Fig. 1.2) calibrated for a 1024×768 display screen, and recorded the last line users can read correctly from 3-ft distance using identical screen for all users. Based on that we can calculate the minimum visual angle required for different users and can convert it into different units of specifying font size like point, pixel or em.

Colour Blindness (CB) We measured the presence and type of color blindness using the plates 16 and 17 of Ishihara Test [7] (Fig. 1.3). People with dichromatic color blindness can only read one digit—people with Protanopia can only read the left hand side digit while with Deuteranopia can only read right hand side digit.

Grip Strength (GS) measures how much force a person can exert gripping with the hand. We measured it using a mechanical dynamometer (Fig. 1.4).

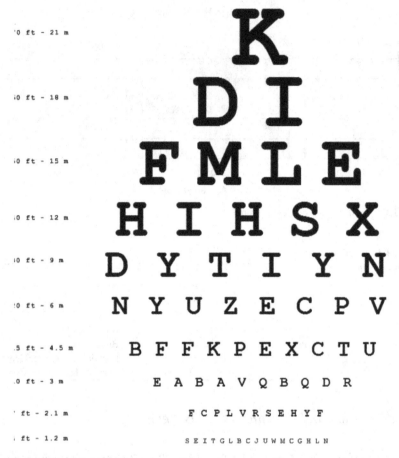

Fig. 1.2 Snellen chart used in the study

Active Range of Motion of Wrist (ROMW) ROMW is measured as the summation of radial and ulnar deviation. Radial deviation is the motion that rotates the wrist away from the midline of the body when the person is standing in the standard anatomical position [12]. When the hand is placed over a table with palm facing down, this motion rotates the hand about the wrist toward the thumb. Ulnar deviation is the motion that rotates the wrist towards the midline of the body when the person is standing in the standard anatomical position. When the hand is placed over a table with palm facing down, this motion rotates the hand about the wrist towards the little finger. We measured the deviations with the goniometer (Fig. 1.5).

Trail Making Test (TMT) The Trail Making Test [2] is a neuropsychological test of visual attention and task switching. It consists of two parts in which the subject is instructed to connect a set of 25 dots as fast as possible while still maintaining accuracy. It can provide information about visual search speed, scanning, speed of

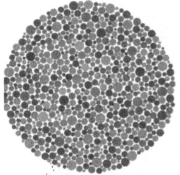

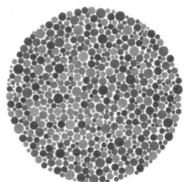

Fig. 1.3 Plates 16 and 17 of Ishihara test

Fig. 1.4 Measuring grip
strength

processing, mental flexibility, as well as executive functioning. It is also sensitive to detecting several cognitive impairments such as Alzheimer's disease and dementia.

Digit Symbol Test (DST) It is a neuropsychological test [2] sensitive to brain damage, dementia, age, and depression. It consists of (e.g. nine) digit-symbol pairs (e.g. 1/-, 2/⊥ … 7/Λ, 8/X, 9/=) followed by a list of digits. Under each digit the subject should write down the corresponding symbol as fast as possible. The number of correct symbols within the allowed time (90 s) is measured.

Besides these objective measurements, we also recorded presence of any particular impairment that may affect users' interaction with electronic interfaces.

1.2.4   Attitude and Experience Towards Technology

We conducted a semi-structured interview and discussion with each user about their experience of using technologies and their attitudes toward new electronic devices like tablet computers or smartphones. We used the following questionnaire to start

Measuring Radial Deviation

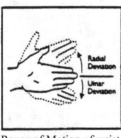

Range of Motion of wrist
(Palm facing down)

Measuring Ulnar Deviation

Fig. 1.5 Measuring active ROM of wrist

discussion, but also allowed users to speak freely about any particular issue or problem they wished to highlight. We took help from local language experts to communicate with users whenever needed.

1. I think that new technological devices are developed mainly to be used by young users.
2. I think that I need to use new technology.
3. I consider it important to try to be open-minded towards new technologies.
4. I consider myself having the necessary skills to manage to use new technological tools.
5. I have problems to using these technologies properly even with practice.
6. The problems with technological devices are impossible to understand, so it is hard to find a solution.
7. When there is a problem with a new technology tool, it is because there is something wrong with that device.
8. I am afraid to touch a new technology tool in case I will break it.
9. I do not get the advantage of using new technological tools.
10. I prefer to use an old fashioned tool with fewer functions than a new one.
11. Do you use

    a. Computer
    b. Tablet
    c. Kiosks, at railway station, community centre
    d. TV
    e. Mobile phone
    f. Smartphone

12. Peripherals used with computer/tablet/TV
13. Problems with computer/laptop
14. Problem with mobile phone
15. Do you have experience with any "special" device?
16. Problem with any other electronic device

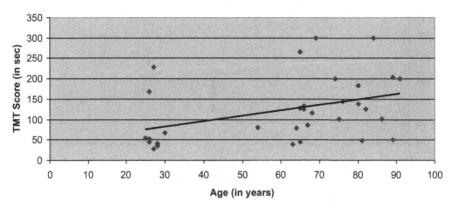

Fig. 1.6 Comparing TMT score with age

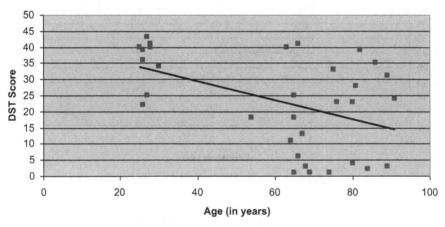

Fig. 1.7 Comparing DST score with age

1.3   Results

1.3.1   Cognitive Data Analysis

We analyzed the effect of age and education on cognitive scores of participants. For the Indian population we found a moderate correlation between age and TMT score ($\rho = 0.38$) and DST Score ($\rho = -0.46$) (Figs. 1.6 and 1.7). However we did not find age to be correlated with TMT and DST scores considering only elderly population; instead education level significantly correlated with TMT ($\rho = -0.68$, $p < 0.01$) and DST scores ($\rho = 0.79$, $p < 0.01$) (Figs. 1.8 and 1.9). The graphs used the following coding scheme for education level (Table 1.2)

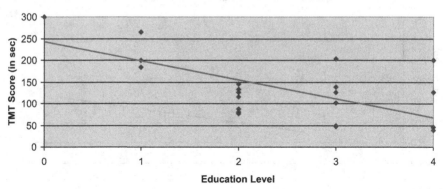

Fig. 1.8 Comparing TMT score with education level

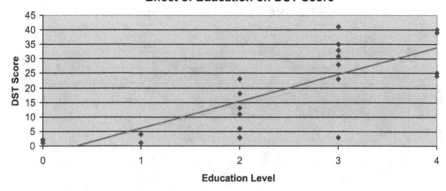

Fig. 1.9 Comparing DST score with education level

We compared the cognitive scores of Indian population with their EU counter-part. We found that TMT and DST scores are significantly different between EU and Indian samples—European people took less time in completing the Trail Making Task and scored more in the Digit Symbol Task than their Indian counterpart. (Tables 1.3 and 1.4)

We also did not find any significant correlation between age, education level and TMT, DST scores for European population (Figs. 1.10 and 1.11).

1.3.2   Hand Strength Data Analysis

We found that age (Fig. 1.12), gender and height have a significant effect on grip strength for Indian population. Table 1.5 shows result from a linear regression to predict grip strength from age, gender and height.

Table 1.2 Coding scheme for education level

Education Level	Code
Illiterate	0
Preschool	1
School	2
Graduate	3
Postgraduate	4

Table 1.3 T-test result on TMT score

	EU_TMT	Indian_TMT
Mean	66.94667	1,22.4375
Variance	1,713.735	6,181.931
Observations	45	32
Hypothesized Mean Difference	0	
df	43	
t Stat	−3.64891	
P(T<=t) one-tail	0.000354	
t Critical one-tail	1.681071	
P(T<=t) two-tail	0.000708	
t Critical two-tail	2.016692	

Table 1.4 T-test result on DST score

	EU_DST	Indian_DST
Mean	39.84444	23.21875
Variance	249.2253	215.9829
Observations	45	32
Hypothesized Mean Difference	0	
df	70	
t Stat	4.742886	
P(T<=t) one-tail	5.38E-06	
t Critical one-tail	1.666914	
P(T<=t) two-tail	1.08E-05	
t Critical two-tail	1.994437	

However, we did not find significant effect of gender and height on a similar linear regression analysis on active ROMW, only age is significantly correlated with ROMW (Fig. 1.13 and Table 1.6).

We compared the hand strength between Indian and EU population. A few European elderly people had grip strength higher than their Indian counterpart, but the ROMW did not have any significant difference (Figs. 1.14 and 1.15).

We have found that for female EU elderly people, grip strength moderately correlates with their age ($\rho = -0.43$) though age was not found to be correlated with Range of Motion of Wrist (Figs. 1.16 and 1.17).

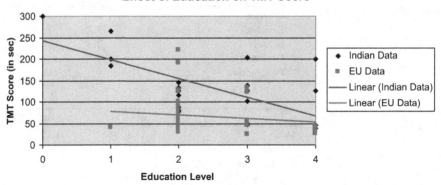

Fig. 1.10 Comparing effect of education level on TMT score between Indian and EU population

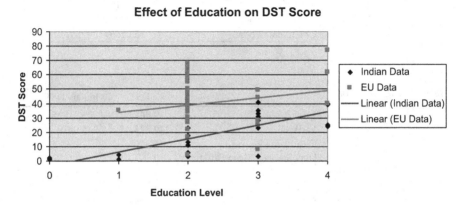

Fig. 1.11 Comparing effect of education level on DST score between Indian and EU population

1.3.3   Visual Data Analysis

Among the Indian population, approximately one-third of the sample needed bigger font size than the standard level. They could not read the 3-m line in a Snellen chart from 3 m distance from screen. A few users who can read the 3-m line from a 3 m distance commented that they will be benefitted with a bigger font size in mobile keypad. We found that 8 among 33 users could not read the plates 16 and 17 of Ishihara color blindness test properly, 5 of them seemed to have Protanopia type of color blindness as they could only read the left hand digit correctly, the other 3 could not read any number at all.

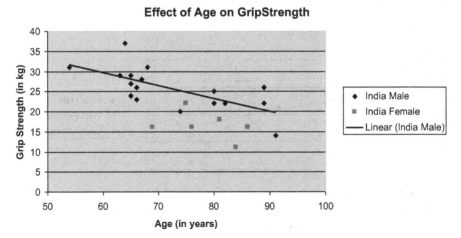

Fig. 1.12 Effect of age on grip strength

Table 1.5 Linear regression to predict grip strength

Regression Statistics				
Multiple R	0.85			
R Square	0.72			
Adjusted R Square	0.67			
Standard Error	3.60			
Observations	23			
ANOVA				
	df	SS	MS	F
Regression	3	621.74	207.25	15.96
Residual	19	246.69	12.98	
Total	22	868.43		
	Coefficients	Standard Error	t Stat	P-value
Intercept	31.69	14.34	2.21	0.04
Age	−0.36	0.08	−4.37	3E-04
Sex	−4.84	2.20	−2.20	0.04
Height	0.15	0.08	1.81	0.086

1.3.4 Attitude Toward Technology Data Analysis

Section 1.2.4. lists the questions used to understand attitude towards technology while Table 1.8 reports the response of people from different countries. Each question had three possible response—Agreed, Disagreed and Neutral.

We did not find any significant difference among elderly people from Spain, UK, India and Germany regarding their attitude towards technology through a single factor ANOVA (Fig. 1.18, Table 1.9). The subjective attitude is discussed in more detail in subsection 4.4.

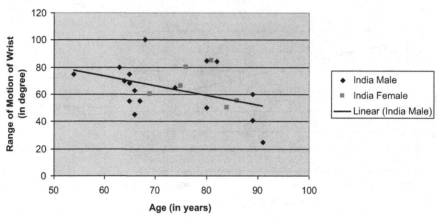

Fig. 1.13 Effect of age on ROMW

Table 1.6 Linear regression to predict active range of motion of wrist (ROMW)

Regression Statistics				
Multiple R	0.50			
R Square	0.25			
Adjusted R Square	0.14			
Standard Error	15.91			
Observations	23			
ANOVA				
	df	SS	MS	F
Regression	3	1,639.68	546.56	2.16
Residual	19	4,810.93	253.21	
Total	22	6,450.61		
	Coefficients	Standard Error	t Stat	P-value
Intercept	17.63	63.32	0.28	0.78
Age	−0.88	0.37	−2.39	0.03
Sex	14.79	9.71	1.52	0.14
Height	0.58	0.37	1.57	0.13

1.3.5 Technology Exposure Data Analysis

We found that none of the Indian users ever used tablet computers, kiosk or smart TV, only a couple of users use smartphones, while all users can use basic call making and receiving facilities of mobile phone and can view their favourite channel on television. Most of the younger people with physical impairment use computers regularly, while three to four elderly users have used computer before though none of the elderly users use computer regularly. They reported that they found computers complicated to use, could not remember functionalities and could not find it useful. However a few users wanted to use computers for emailing their sons or daughter or pursuing their hobbies like cookery, knitting, etc.

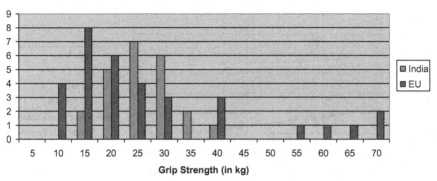

Fig. 1.14 Comparing grip strength histogram between Indian and EU populations

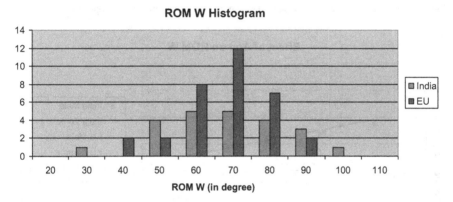

Fig. 1.15 Comparing ROMW histogram between Indian and EU populations

1.4   Discussion

The aim of this survey was to understand effect of age on capability and attitude towards technology, in particular electronic interactive devices like computer, TV, mobile phone and so on. The study has pointed out some interesting insights as pointed below.

1.4.1   Education Level is More Important Than Age with Respect to Cognition

We found that age has a moderate correlation with TMT and DST scores even considering younger users, but education level has a significant correlation in retaining task switching capabilities or retaining visual attention or short-term memory as reflected and measured by the cognitive tests.

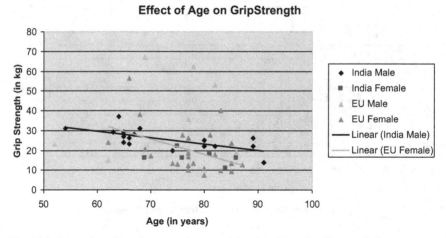

Fig. 1.16 Comparing effect of age on grip strength between EU and Indian populations

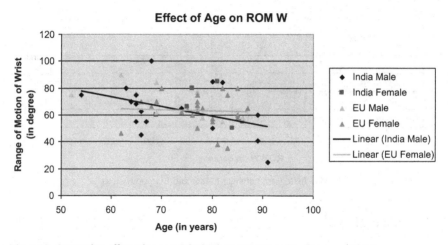

Fig. 1.17 Comparing effect of age on ROMW between EU and Indian populations

Designers should consider the education level of their intended users while designing screen layouts, as a screen with many items may confuse users with lower education level. This issue becomes more relevant while designing applications for illiterate or neo-literate people in India.

We also found that the average scores in cognitive tests are higher in European population. One possible reason may be most European users had a minimum level of school education, while that was not true for their Indian counterparts (Fig. 1.19).

Table 1.7 List of questions used to assess attitude towards technology

1	I think that new technology devices are developed mainly to be used by young users
2	I think that I need to use new technology
3	I consider it important to try to be open-minded towards new technology
4	I consider myself having the necessary skills to manage to use new technology tools
5	I have problems to use these technologies properly even with practice
6	The problems of technology devices are impossible to understand, so it is hard to find a solution
7	When there is a problem with a new technology tool, it is because there is something wrong with that device
8	I am afraid to touch a new technology tool in case I will break it
9	I don't get advantage of using new technology tools
10	I prefer to use an old fashion tool with fewer functions than a new one

Table 1.8 Response from users from different countries

	% of users Agreed			
Question No.	Spain	UK	Germany	India
1	30.8	56	46.7	30.43
2	26.9	60	68.8	69.23
3	84.6	72	100	92.31
4	42.3	16	37.5	39.13
5	15.4	56	25	46.15
6	42.3	68	75	15.38
7	15.4	44	31.3	15.38
8	42.3	40	12.5	30.43
9	30.8	54.2	18.8	53.85
10	57.7	68	56.3	52.17

	% of users Disagreed			
Question No.	Spain	UK	Germany	India
1	69.2	20	40	65.22
2	46.2	28	0	23.08
3	7.7	4	0	0
4	23.1	48	31.3	47.83
5	61.5	28	56.3	30.77
6	30.8	12	12.5	46.15
7	42.3	32	50	53.85
8	38.5	40	68.8	65.22
9	61.5	37.5	68.8	30.77
10	23.1	28	25	47.83

1.4.2 Age Reduces Hand Strength in Turn Capability of Using Computer Peripherals

Our previous study [3, 4] found that grip strength and active range of motion of wrist is indicative of users' pointing performance with a variety of pointing devices

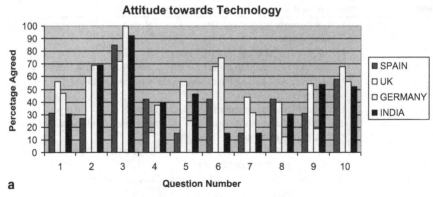

Fig. 1.18 Comparing attitudes towards technology for different users. **a** Comparing users agreed to question statements. **b** Comparing users disagreed to question statements

Table 1.9 ANOVA results on users' response

ANOVA on users agreed to question statements					
ANOVA Summary					
Source	SS	df	MS	F	P
Group	1,100.08	3	366.69	0.71	0.55
Error	18,480.70	36	513.35		
Total	19,580.78	39			
ANOVA on uses disagreed to question statements					
Group	1,135.35	3	378.45	0.92	0.44
Error	14,793.70	36	410.94		
Total	15,929.04	39			

like mouse, trackball, touch screen and stylus. We found that both Indian and EU population reduce their grip strength with age that effectively make their use of standard computer peripherals inefficient. The reduced hand strength also makes it difficult to use touch screen or keypads which was also explicitly mentioned by a few participants.

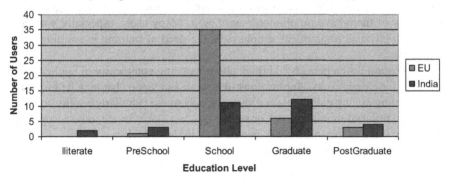

Fig. 1.19 Comparing education level of Indian and EU samples

Designers and interface developers should explore use of hands-free control for elderly users. Eye-gaze tracking [5] or brain–computer interfaces [5] can offer valuable alternatives to standard keyboard, mouse and touch screen interfaces.

Our analysis also developed a model to predict grip strength from age, height and gender of participants which was reported earlier in ergonomics literature [1] but not probably validated on Indian population.

1.4.3   Bigger Font Size and Buttons Are Good

We found that one-third of users had reduced visual acuity even with a corrective glass. However most elderly users used glasses and a few of them more than one for near and far vision. It is likely that they may use the TV or mobile phone without their glasses or with the wrong glasses on. Their reduced visual acuity compounded with reduced hand strength limits usability of standard mobile or remote keypad as well standard computer or TV interfaces.

Designers should provide bigger buttons and font sizes for elderly people. They should also adjust color contrast for users with color blindness.

1.4.4   Elderly Users Will Use it if it is Interesting and Easy to Use

Most of our elderly users use the basic functionalities of mobile phone and TV as they find it easy to use and useful. However that does not hold true for computers as they find it complicated and serving no useful purpose for them. Some elderly users relied on others to send emails to their distant relatives. However more than 60 % users in India and Spain believed that new technology was not only meant for young users and more than 80 % of them felt themselves open-minded to use new technology. More than 60 % of Indian, British and German elderly users wanted to use new technology. However the opinion about braking a new tool or using old-fashion tools is not very obvious as on average 50 % users agree or disagree to it and a few of them have no opinion regarding it. Many users, especially younger ones with physical impairment, emphasized the need of training in learning new technology.

Application developers should think about reducing complexity of applications intended for elderly users. Applications like email and video chat may be found to be interesting among elderly users if they are easy to use. Similarly application deployed on low-end mobile phones or set top box has more chance to be acceptable by elderly users as they are already accustomed to those devices.

1.4.5   Conclusions

This chapter reports results from a survey on capability and attitude towards technology of elderly users conducted at three different geographic locations in India. The paper also compares results of a similar survey conducted in Spain, Germany and UK. The survey finds important results in terms of hand strength and cognitive abilities of users. It proposes a model to predict grip strength from age, sex and height of Indian elderly people while also reports a significant effect of education on scores of cognitive tests. Comparative analysis with European elderly people shows that European people tend to sustain better cognitive abilities with age though their attitude towards new technology is not significantly different from their Indian counterpart. Finally it reports subjective view of elderly people about technology and proposes guidelines for future interface designers in developing countries. The following chapters have utilized the survey in developing a user model and proposing new interfaces and interaction techniques.

References

1. Angst, F., et al. (2010). Prediction of grip and key pinch strength in 978 healthy subjects. BMC Musculoskeletal Disorders, 11, 94.
2. Army Individual Test Battery. (1944). Manual of directions and scoring. D.C. War Department, Adjuvant General's Office: Washington.
3. Biswas, P., & Langdon, P. (2012) Developing multimodal adaptation algorithm for mobility impaired users by evaluating their hand strength. International Journal of Human-Computer Interaction, 28(9), 576–596, (Taylor & Francis, Print ISSN: 1044-7318).
4. Biswas P., & Robinson P. (2009) Predicting pointing time from hand strength, usability & HCI for e-Inclusion, 5th symposium of the Austrian computer society (USAB 2009). Berlin: Springer.
5. Biswas, P., Joshi, R., Chattopadhyay, S., Acharya, U. R., & Lim, T. (2013) Interaction techniques for users with severe motor-impairment. . P. Biswas, C. Duarte, P. Langdon, L. Alameda, & C. Jung (Eds.), A multimodal end-2-end approach to accessible computing (pp. 119–135). Berlin: Springer.

6. Biswas, P., & Robinson, P., & Langdon P. (2012) Designing inclusive interfaces through user modelling and simulation. *International Journal of Human-Computer Interaction, 28*(1), 1–33, (Taylor & Francis, Print ISSN: 1044-7318).

7. Colour Blindness Test (2008). http://www.kcl.ac.uk/teares/gktvc/vc/lt/colourblindness/cblind.htm. Accessed 12 Aug2008.

8. Dalstra, J. A. A., Kunst, A. E., Borrell, C., Breeze, E., Cambois, E., Costa, G., et al. (2005). Socioeconomic differences in the prevalence of common chronic diseases: An overview of eight European countries. *International Journal of Epidemiology, 34*(2), 316–326.

9. GUIDE D7.1. (2013) Initial user study. http://www.guide-project.eu/includes/requestFile.php?id=129&pub=2. Accessed 18 June 2013.

10. ITU (2013) Making Mobile Phones and Services accessible for Persons with Disabilities. http://www.itu.int/ITU-D/sis/PwDs/Documents/Mobile_Report.pdf. Accessed 18 June 2013.

11. ITU (2013) Making Television Accessible Report. G3ict-ITU, November 2011. http://www.itu.int/ITU-D/sis/PwDs/Documents/Making_TV_Accessible-FINAL-WithAltTextInserted.pdf. Accessed 18 June 2013.

12. Kaplan, R. J. (2006). *Physical medicine and rehabilitation review.* New York: McGraw Hill.

13. Langdon, P., & Thimbleby, H. (2010). Inclusion and interaction: Designing interaction for inclusive populations. *Interacting with computers, V22* (pp. 439–448). Amsterdam: Elsevier (Editorial for special edition).

14. Mackenbach, J. P., et al. (1997). Socioeconomic inequalities in morbidity and mortality in Western Europe. *Lancet, 349*(9066), 1655–1659.

15. Siegrist J., & Marmot M. (2004). Health inequalities and the psychosocial environment—two scientific challenges. *Social Science & Medicine, 58*(8), 1463–1473.

Chapter 2
User Model

Poster Boy - presenting user model at Research Council UK's meeting in Delhi

2.1   Introduction

User model can be defined as a machine-readable representation of user character-istics of a system. We have developed a user model that considers users with physi-cal, age-related or contextual impairment and can be used to personalize electronic interfaces to facilitate human–machine interaction. We have identified a set of hu-man factors that can affect human–computer interaction, and formulated models [2] to relate those factors to interface parameters. We have developed inclusive user model, which can adjust font size, font colour, inter-element spacing (like line

P. Biswas, *Inclusive Human Machine Interaction for India,*   21
Human–Computer Interaction Series, DOI 10.1007/978-3-319-06500-7_2,
© Springer International Publishing Switzerland 2014

spacing, button spacing, etc.) based on age, gender, visual acuity, type of colour blindness, presence of hand tremor and spasm of users. The model is more detailed than GOMS model [9], easier to use than cognitive architecture-based models [1, 14], and covers a wider range of users than existing user models for disabled users. The user profile is created using a web form and the profile is stored in cloud. Once created, this profile is accessible to the user irrespective of application and device.

The user modelling process started with a survey on users with physical and age related impairment. The survey was not exhaustive but still found out requirements and problems of elderly users, while using existing electronic systems. We formulated a user model to solve a few of these issues. The user model took help from our previous work on inclusive user modelling. This new user model is implemented like an application and device agnostic web service. We have worked with different development teams to integrate this user model into their applications. In parallel we conducted user trials to validate the user model. Finally, we were able to integrate this user modelling web service with a few applications and conducted user trial to evaluate the efficacy of the adaptive system.

2.2   User Modelling Framework

The user survey was conducted only on 33 users. The statistical results may need further validation with more data but the subjective trends lead to specific user requirements. Almost all users preferred bigger font sizes in electronic interfaces and one-third of them had colour blindness. It was also noted that elderly users found existing computing applications complicated, but they will use a system if it is simple to learn and use. We also found a gradual decline of grip strength and active range of motion of wrist of elderly users, as they turned older, resulting reduced control of precise wrist movements.

We have tried to address these uses through the inclusive user modelling system. Existing challenges with user models are

- Having an application-agnostic format
- Compatibility to multiple applications
- Integration to multiple applications
- Relating human factor to interface parameters
- Collecting representative human factors to personalize interface

We have developed the Inclusive User Model and used it to develop a user modelling web service that can automatically adjust font size, colour contrast, line and button spacing of interfaces based on visual acuity, type of colour blindness, grip strength, active range of motion of wrist and static tremor of users. The user modelling system addressed the above issues in the following way.

The user modelling system:

- Follows a standardized user profile format specified by an EU cluster [11] and published by International Telecommunication Union [8]

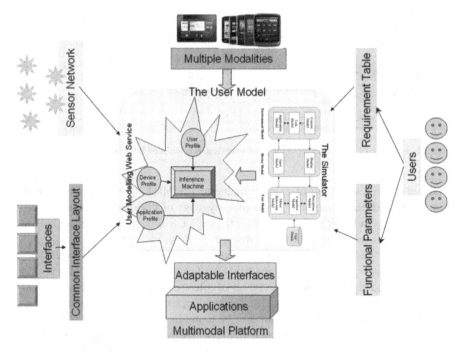

Fig. 2.1 Personalization framework

- Does not propose to change content of an interface rather specifies layout parameters, so it is easily integrated to different applications
- Can automatically convert interface parameters (like font size or button spacing) for multiple devices (e.g. TV, computer, laptop, mobile phone etc.) by assuming a viewing distance for different devices and taking the screen resolution as input parameter [6]
- Has investigated details of visual, auditory and motor functions of humans and is developed through extensive user trials to relate human factors to interface parameters [2–6]

Figure 2.1 illustrates a diagram of the personalization framework. The framework takes input about users' functional parameters (like visual acuity, colour blindness, short-term memory capacity, first language and dexterity level) and subjective requirements. These requirements are fed into the Inclusive User Model that consists of perception, cognition and motor-behaviour models. The Inclusive User Model can predict how a person with visual acuity v and contrast sensitivity s will perceive an interface or a person with grip strength g and range of motion of wrist (ROMW) w will use a pointing device.

Figure 2.2 shows an example of the output from Inclusive User Model. Figure 2.2a shows the original interface. Figure 2.2b shows the perception and probable cursor trace for a user with protanopia colour blindness, early stage of dry macular degeneration and Parkinson's disease. The colour contrast of Fig. 2.2b is

Fig. 2.2 Example of the simulator. a Original interface. b Simulated interface

changed to simulate effect of colour blindness. The black spots and overall blur-ring is resulted due to simulate effect of early stage of dry macular degeneration. The blue (gray in B&W) line shows how the cursor will move for a person having tremor of the hand due to Parkinson's disease.

The survey described in the previous chapter generated the range of visual acu-ity, colour blindness, grip strength and ROMW of users. This range of values is used in Monte Carlo simulation to predict a set of rules relating users' range of abilities with interface parameters like font size, colour contrast, line spacing, default zoom-ing level, etc. Detail on the simulator can be found in separate papers [3, 4], while a set of rules can be found in the Appendix. The rule-based system along with user, device and application profiles is stored in a cloud-based server (Fig. 2.1). The cli-ent application can access the web service using a plug-in.

The framework is integrated to applications using a client application. The client application reads data from the user model and sensor network and changes the font size, font colour, line spacing, default zooming level and so on by either selecting an appropriate pre-defined stylesheet or changing parameters for each individual webpage or standalone application.

Figure 2.3 below shows four different renderings of a weather monitoring system for people with different range of visual and motor impairments. The system is part of the WISEKAR system [16] developed at the Indian Institute of Technology, Delhi. All these figures are reporting temperature and humidity data of different cities with possible extension to show pollution data as well. The system changes the foreground colour to blue and background colour to yellow for users having red-green colour blindness (Fig. 2.3b). It uses bigger font size and turn on high-contrast for people having blurred or distorted vision due to severe myopia, macular degeneration or diabetic retinopathy (Fig. 2.3c). Finally the system also adjusts the default zooming level and line spacing, if the user has tremor or spasm in hand. A higher zooming level separates screen elements to reduce chances of wrong selection (Fig. 2.3d).

The system has also been integrated to an agriculture advisory system that pro-motes use of technology to increase the agricultural efficiency by providing farm-specific, crop-specific advisory to farmers. The agriculture advisory system has two components:

- The Pest–Disease Image Upload (PDIU) application is used by farmers to up-load images of infested crops, while they are in the field. The uploaded images

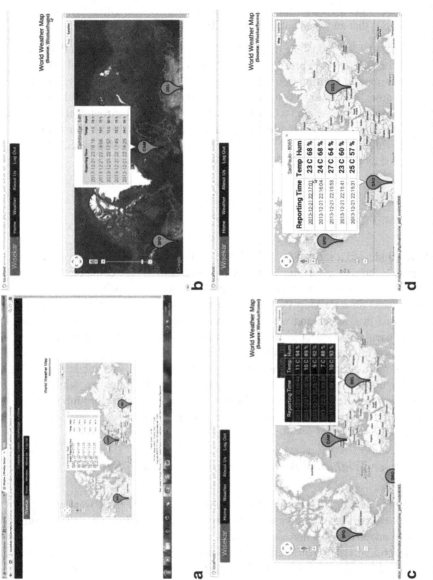

Fig. 2.3 Personalized weather-monitoring system. **a** Non Adapted. **b** Adapted for red-green colour-blind. **c** Adapted for blurred vision. **d** Adapted for blurred vision and hand tremor

are automatically sent to remotely located experts, who advise farmers about remedy. The application runs on low-end mobile phones or smart phones. It not only makes it easy for farmers who have difficulty in operating a keypad but also accommodates those suffering from poor vision or cognitive impairments.

- A web-based Dashboard system runs on a personal computer and is used by experts to advice farmers. Experts can be across all age levels, and it is, therefore, important to design a user interface that takes into account impairments of different kinds that an expert might possibly be dealing with.

Figures 2.4 and 2.5 demonstrate different rendering of the Dashboard and PDIU applications for different user profiles. This system is developed at the Rural Technology and Business Incubation Centre of the Indian Institute of Technology, Madras.

The weather monitoring system can be found at http://wisekar.iitd.ernet.in/wisekar_mm/index.php/main, while the eAgri system can be found at http://e-vivasaya.rtbi.in/aas_cambridge/login.php. Renderings similar to the above can be generated with usernames user-1, user-2, user-3, user-4, etc. In each case, the password is same as the username.

2.3   User Trials

We have conducted a series of user trials to validate the adaptive interfaces generated through the user modeling web service. The first trial [2] conducted an icon searching task involving users with age-related and physical impairment. The study was conducted on a desktop PC and a tablet computer using different organizations of icons in a screen and with and without integrating the user model. It was found that users could select icons quicker and with less error when the screen was adapted following the prediction of user model.

The second user study [5] evaluated the prediction of the user model for situational impairment using a text searching task on a tablet computer, while users were walking in a field. Again it was found that a screen adapted through the user model was quicker to use and produced fewer errors.

2.3.1   User Trial on Wisekar Weather Monitoring System

The following user trial reports a controlled experiment on a real life weather monitoring application. It compared users' objective performance and subjective preference for an adaptive and a nonadaptive versions of the weather monitoring system. We purposefully used two different devices for signing up and using the application to highlight the notion of transporting user profile across multiple devices.

Fig. 2.4 Different renderings of the Dashboard application

Fig. 2.5 Different renderings of the PDIU application

Table 2.1 List of participants

Participant	Age	Gender	Impairment
P1	60	Male	+2.5 Dioptre power
P2	57	Male	−2.5 Dioptre power
P3	59	Male	+2.5 Dioptre power
P4	42	Male	5/6 vision
P5	50	Female	+1 Dioptre power
P6	57	Male	Recently operated cataract, blurred vision
P7	59	Male	+1.5 Dioptre power

2.3.1.1   Participants

We collected data from users with age-related visual or motor impairment. Table 2.1 furnishes details of participants. The study was conducted at Delhi, India.

2.3.1.2   Material

We have used a Windows 7 HP computer with 54 cm×33 cm monitor having 1920 × 1080 pixels resolution to record users' performance with the weather monitoring system. We used a standard Logitech mouse for pointing. Users signed up using a HP T×2 laptop with 30 cm×20 cm screen and 1280×800 pixels resolution.

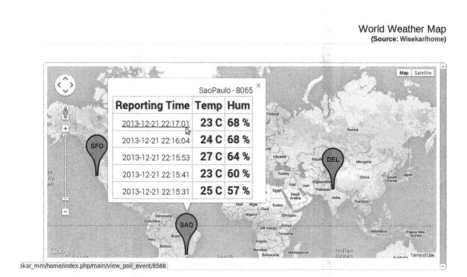

Fig. 2.6 Screenshots of WISEKAR weather monitoring system

2.3.1.3   Procedure

The participants were initially registered with the user modelling system using the Laptop. The sign-up page can be accessed at www-edc.eng.cam.ac.uk/~pb400/ CambUM/UMSignUp.htm.

After that, participants were briefed about the weather monitoring system. The task was to report temperature and humidity of cities on a specific date (Fig. 2.6). Each participant was instructed to report temperature and humidity six times for each of adapted and nonadapted conditions. The order of adapted and nonadapted conditions was altered randomly to eliminate order effect.

2.3.1.4   Results

During the sign-up stage, we found that different users preferred different font sizes ranging from 14 to 18 points. We also noticed that one user was protanomalous colour blind and he read 45 instead of 42 in the plate 16 of Ishihara colour blindness test.

During the use of the weather monitoring system, we measured the time interval between pressing the left mouse button on the bubble with the city name (round shape in Fig. 2.7a) and reporting of the required temperature and humidity data (Fig. 2.7b).

In total, we analysed 84 tasks (42 for adapted and 42 for nonadapted). We found that users took significantly less time in adapted condition (average 8.25 s, stan-

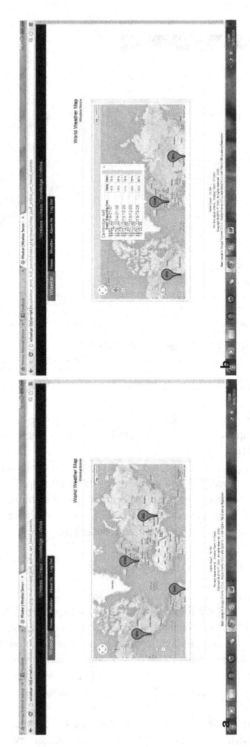

Fig. 2.7 The experimental task. **a** The screenshot shown to user for selecting city. **b** The weather reporting screen

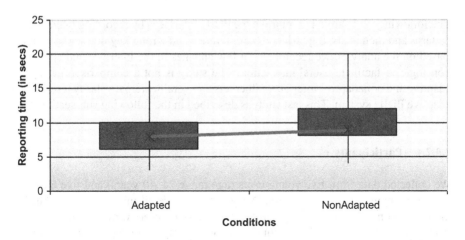

Fig. 2.8 Comparing weather reporting times

dard deviation 3.1 s) than nonadapted condition (average 9.75 s, standard deviation 3.63 s). All participants were already familiar with mouse and also practiced the system before the actual trial. So we assumed that each pointing task was independent to each other. Under this assumption, the difference is significant in a two-tailed paired t-test with $p < 0.05$ and with an effect size (Cohen's d) of 0.44 (Fig. 2.8).

Without this assumption, the difference is significant in Wilcoxon signed-rank test ($Z = -2.1, p < 0.05$).

We conducted a subjective questionnaire to understand users' subjective preference. All users noticed bigger font and preferred it. One user was colour-blind and he preferred the change in colour contrast too.

2.3.1.5   Discussion

The user study shows that users prefer different font sizes and colour contrast even for a simple system. The study also confirms that even for a simple text searching task, users performed and preferred an adaptive system that can automatically adjusts font size, line spacing and colour contrast. The user modeling system successfully converted users' preference across two different devices having different screen resolutions. Future studies will collect data from more users and will use more complicated tasks than the present study.

2.3.2   User Trial on PDIU Agriculture Advisory System

The following study aimed to improve the PDIU interfaces by recording interaction patterns and then analysing task completion times and wrong key presses by users. Based on the analysis, we recommend a few changes in the interface and application logic to facilitate users' interaction. The study is not a comparison between adaptive and nonadaptive interface, rather it is an overall external validity test of the adaptive PDIU system. This last study is described in the following sub-sections.

2.3.2.1   Participants

We collected data from five young users (age range 24–40 years) and five elderly users (age range 56–65 years) from Mandi. They were all male, related to farming profession and use low-end mobile phones. Young users were educated above matriculation level. One of the young users needed big font size and one had protanopia colour blindness. Elderly users' education levels vary from high school to matriculation. All elderly users preferred biggest text size and two had colour blindness. They can all read English words used in the PDIU interfaces. The study was conducted at Mandi, India.

2.3.2.2   Material

The study was conducted on a Nokia 301 mobile phone.

2.3.2.3   Procedure

The task involved taking photographs of three leaves arranged on a desk using the PDIU application. At first, they were registered to the application. The system then asked their preferred font size and conducted the Ishihara colour blindness test [5] using plate number 16. Based on their response, the application adapted itself, and users were asked if they found the screen legible. Then they were demonstrated the task of taking photographs and after they understood it, they were requested to do the same. The experimenter recorded a video of the interaction. During the task, users needed to go through the screenshots shown in Fig. 2.9. The sequence of actions were as follows:

1. Select PDIU from PDIU home screen (Fig. 2.9a).
2. Scroll down to Open Camera under Image 1 (Fig. 2.9b).
3. Select OpenCamera and take a photograph.
4. Scroll down to Open Camera under Image 2 (Fig. 2.9b).
5. Select OpenCamera and take a photograph.
6. Scroll down to Open Camera under Image 3 (Fig. 2.9c).

Fig. 2.9 PDIU interfaces used in the study. **a** PDIU home screen. **b** Open camera screen. **c** Menu
screen

7. Select OpenCamera and take a photograph.
8. Press Menu (Fig.. 2.9c).
9. Scroll Down to Save option (Fig. 2.9c).
10. Select Save (Fig. 2.9c).

After they completed the task, we conducted a general unstructured interview about
their farming experience and utility of the system.

2.3.2.4   Results

The following graphs (Figs. 2.10 and 2.11) plot the task completion times for the
operations involving taking three pictures and saving them. In these figures, C1–C5
stands for young participants while P1–P5 stands for their elderly counterpart. An
one factor ANOVA found a significant effect of type of tasks among all ten participants ($F(3, 36) = 4.05$, $p < 0.05$). Users took only 21.9 s on average to record the
first image while they took 51.2 s on average to record the second image, 48.4 s on
average to record the third image and 50.7 s on average to go to the Menu and press
Save button.

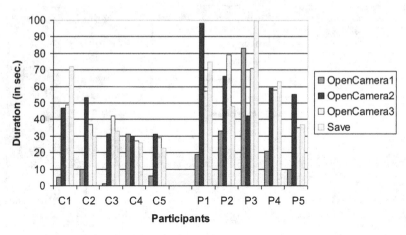

Fig. 2.10 Task completion times for participants

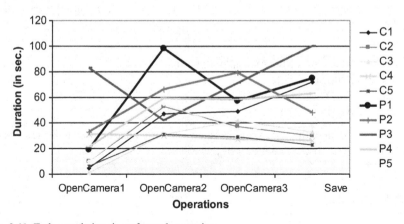

Fig. 2.11 Task completion times for each operation

We also analysed all instances of wrong key presses and Table 2.2 lists them with respect to each participant. In Table 2.2, C1–C5 stands for young participants, while P1–P5 stands for their elderly counterpart.

During the open structured interview, it emerged that they belonged to different sections of the society. They were farmers, landlords, part-time farmers of their ancestral agrarian land pursuing another profession like bus driving. They mostly harvested crops like corn, maize, bajra, wheat, etc. One of their major problems was

Table 2.2 Lists of wrong selection

Participants	Wrong key presses
C1	Went back from OpenCamera2 to OpenCamera1, scrolled up instead of down, recovered himself
	Cancelled Save option was confused but then recovered and finished successfully
C2	Pressed middle button to select the PDIU in home screen
	Selected OpenCamera1 second time instead of scrolling to OpenCamera2
C3	No wrong key press
C4	Scrolling up instead of scrolling down before reaching OpenCamera buttons
C5	Pressed Submit instead of selecting Save had trouble between selection and scroll down buttons
P1	Scrolling up instead of scrolling down before reaching OpenCamera buttons
	Pressed Back button instead of Selecting OpenCamera2
	Pressed Back button again in the PDIU home screen
	Pressed Back button again instead of Selecting OpenCamera2
	Could not scroll down to Save button in Menu items
P2	Pressed middle button of Scroll Button instead of selecting Capture in OpenCamera2
	Pressed Menu instead of going to OpenCamera3
P3	Pressed Back button in PDIU Home Screen
	Pressed Back button from the OpenCamera Screen
	Pressed Back button again from the OpenCamera Screen
	Pressed Left button instead of Middle button in one system message screen
	Pressed OpenCamera1 second time instead of scrolling down to OpenCamera2 button
	Pressed Back button instead of capturing image in OpenCamera3
	Scrolled up to OpenCamera2 from OpenCamera3
	Scrolled down from Save button but then get back to Save button
P4	Pressed middle button instead of Capture button in OpenCamera2
P5	No wrong key press

the quality of grains. One of them reported problem with harvesting corn, which often suffered from disease resulting in white ends and less grain than usual. Another one complained about wheat, which suffered from a disease causing dried stalks. They face massive problems in farming, as they do not get enough modern equipment for harvesting good quality crops. One of them reported about a help centre in their capital town, but it was nearly a hundred kilometers away from their farming place with no good public transportation available. So they hardly could get help from them.

2.3.2.5 Discussion

The farmers found the system useful and the interfaces were legible and comprehensible to them. However some of them, especially the elderly ones, faced problem in scrolling and recovering from error. It seemed to us, a simpler interface will be more useful to the elderly users. Based on the study and list of errors, we propose the following recommendations.

a. Initial focus on OpenCamera Screen

This initial focus can alleviate a few scrolling errors, as users will understand that they need to scroll down to select the open Camera buttons.

b. Only one OpenCamera button with automatic Save option

The ANOVA shows that users were significantly slower in taking the second or third photograph and saving them. If there is only one OpenCamera button which automatically saves or submits the picture, a lot of scrolling errors can be avoided and the overall task completion time will also reduce significantly.

c. Confirmation of Back action in middle of interaction

We found users were often confused if they pressed the Back button. It may be useful to add a confirmation dialog if they press the Back button in the middle of taking a photograph or saving it.

d. Overridden buttons while capturing images

Users pressed the middle button to capture image, which is a common feature in most mobile phones with a camera. It will be a good idea to let users do so making the system more intuitive.

2.4   Related Work

This section presents a brief overview of user models developed for people with physical and age-related impairment. The EASE tool [13] simulates effects of interaction for a few visual and mobility impairments. However the model is demonstrated for a sample application of using a word prediction software but not yet validated for basic pointing or visual search tasks performed by people with disabilities. Keates and colleagues [12] measured the difference between able-bodied and motor-impaired users with respect to the Model Human Processor (MHP) [9] and motor-impaired users were found to have a greater motor action time than their able-bodied counterparts. The finding is obviously important, but the KLM model itself is too primitive to model complex interaction and especially the performance of novice users. Serna and colleagues [17] used ACT-R cognitive architecture [1] to model progress of Dementia in Alzheimer's patient. They simulated the loss of memory and increase in error for a representative task at kitchen by changing different ACT-R parameters [1]. The technique is interesting but their model still needs rigorous validation through other tasks and user communities. The CogTool system [10] combines GOMS models and ACT-R system for providing quantitative prediction on interaction. The system simulates expert performance through GOMS modelling, while the ACT-R system helps to simulate exploratory behaviour of novice users. The system also provides GUIs to quickly prototype interfaces and to evaluate different design alternatives based on quantitative prediction. However it does not yet seem to be used for users with disability or assistive interaction techniques. Quade's [15] simulation uses a probabilistic rule-based system to predict the effect of sensory or motor impairment on design, but it does not model the detail of perceptual and motor abilities like our simulation system. The probabilistic rule-based system does not seem to be validated for users with age-related and different types of physical impairment (visual, hearing and motor) like our system. User model-based interface personalization is mainly explored in the domain of content personalization and developing intelligent information filtering or recommendation systems based on user profiles. In most of those systems, content (or information) is represented in a graph like structure (e.g. ontology or semantic network) and filtering or recommendation is generated by storing and analyzing users' interaction patterns. Little research work has been done beyond content personalization. The SUPPLE project [7] personalizes interfaces mainly by changing layout and font size for people with visual and motor impairment and also for ubiquitous devices. However, the user models do not consider visual and motor impairment in detail and thus work for only loss of visual acuity and a few types of motor impairment. The AVANTI project [18] provides a multimedia web browser for people with light or severe motor disabilities, and blind people. It distinguishes personalization into two classes—static adaptation which is personalization based on user profile and dynamic adaptation that is personalization following the interaction pattern (e.g. calculating error rate, user idle time etc., from usage log) with the system.

The lack of a generalized framework for personalization of users with a wide range of abilities affects the scalability of products as the existing systems work only for a small segment of the user population. For example, there are numerous guidelines [19] and systems for developing accessible websites but they are not always adequate to provide accessibility. Moreover designers often do not conform to the guidelines while developing new systems and design non-inclusive applications. It is also difficult to change existing systems to meet the guidelines. There are a few systems (e.g. IBM Web Adaptation Technology, AVANTI Web browser; 18) which offer features to make web sites accessible, but either they serve a very special type of user (motor-impaired for AVANTI) or there is no way to relate the inclusive features with the particular need of users.

2.5 Conclusions

This chapter presents an application of a user modeling system that is used to store a user profile online and uses it to adapt user interfaces across different applications running on different devices. The detail of the user model itself was published earlier. This chapter describes the integration of the user modeling system with multiple applications and reports a user trial to validate the adaptive system. The user model also follows a standardized format to store the profile, so that it can be easily integrated to multiple applications developed by different development teams. Our user studies confirm that systems adapted by the user modeling system are preferred by users and it also statistically significantly reduces task completion times.

References

1. Anderson, J. R., & Lebiere, C. (1998). *The atomic components of thought.* Hillsdale: Lawrence Erlbaum Associates.
2. Biswas, P., & Langdon, P. (2013). Validating User Modelling Web Service, W3C User Modelling for Accessibility (UM4A) Online Symposium
3. Biswas, P., & Langdon, P. (2013). Inclusive user modeling and simulation. In P. Biswas et al. (Eds.), *A multimodal end-2-end approach to accessible computing* (pp. 71–92). London: Springer.
4. Biswas, P., & Langdon, P. (2012). Inclusive user modelling and simulation. *Advances in therapeutic engineering* (pp. 283–306). Oxford: CRC press.
5. Biswas, P., Langdon, P., Umadikar, J., Kittusami, S., & Prashant, S. (2014). How interface adaptation for physical impairment can help able bodied users in situational impairment. *Joining usability, accessibility, and inclusion* (pp. 49–58). Cham: Springer International
6. Biswas, P., Robinson, P., & Langdon, P. (2012). Designing inclusive interfaces through user modelling and simulation. *International Journal of Human-Computer Interaction, 28*(1), 1–33 (Taylor & Francis, Print ISSN: 1044–7318).
7. Gajos, K. Z., Wobbrock, J. O., & Weld, D. S. (2007). Automatically generating user interfaces adapted to users' motor and vision capabilities. *ACM symposium on user interface software and technology* (pp. 231–240). Boca Raton: CRC Press.
8. ITU Technical Report of the Focus Group on Smart Cable Television. (2013). http://www.itu.int/dms_pub/itu-t/opb/fg/T-FG-SMART-2013-PDF-E.pdf. Accessed 25 Jan 2013.
9. John, B. E., & Kieras, D. (1996). The GOMS family of user interface analysis techniques: Comparison and contrast. *ACM Transactions on Computer Human Interaction, 3,* 320–351.
10. John, B. E. (2010). Reducing the Variability between Novice Modelers: Results of a Tool for Human Performance Modelling Produced through Human-Centered Design. Behavior Representation in Modelling and Simulation (BRIMS).
11. Kaklanis, N. et al. (2012). An interoperable and inclusive user modelling concept for simulation and adaptation. International Conference on User Modeling (UMAP).
12. Keates, S., Clarkson, J., & Robinson, P. (2000). Investigating the applicability of user models for motion impaired users. ACM/SIGACCESS Conference on Computers and Accessibility. pp. 129–136.
13. Mankoff, J., Fait, H., & Juang, R. (2005). Evaluating accessibility through simulating the experiences of users with vision or motor impairments. *IBM Systems Journal, 44*(3), 505–518.
14. Newell, A. (1990). *Unified theories of cognition.* Cambridge: Harvard University Press.
15. Quade, M. et al. (2011). Evaluating User Interface Adaptations at Runtime by Simulating User Interaction. British HCI.
16. Sarangi, S., & Kar, S. (2013). Wireless Sensor Knowledge Archive, Proceedings of the International Conference on Electronics, Computing and Communication Technologies (IEEE CONECCT), Bangalore, Jan 17–19.
17. Serna, A., Pigot, H., & Rialle, V. (2007). Modeling the progression of Alzheimer's disease for cognitive assistance in smart homes. *User Modeling and User-Adapted Interaction, 17*(4), 415–438.
18. Stephanidis, C. et al. (1998). Adaptable and Adaptive User Interfaces for Disabled Users in the AVANTI Project. Intelligence in Services And Networks, LNCS-1430, Springer-Verlag.
19. WAI Guidelines and Techniques. (2012) http://www.w3.org/WAI/guid-tech.html. Accessed 4 Dec 2012.

Chapter 3
User Interaction

Convincing future technocrats - kids trying out eye-gaze tracker at IIT Bombay
TechFest

3.1 Introduction

The previous chapter proposes a user model to personalize existing interfaces. However, we can think beyond personalization to facilitate human–machine interaction. The survey in Chap. 1 pointed out that few elderly users found it difficult to operate a mouse or found the buttons on a TV remote too small to touch. This chapter proposes new interaction modalities involving eye-gaze and head movement trackers.

P. Biswas, *Inclusive Human Machine Interaction for India,*
Human–Computer Interaction Series, DOI 10.1007/978-3-319-06500-7_3,
© Springer International Publishing Switzerland 2014

In particular, this chapter presents a neural-network-based model to predict pointing target that has been tested with three different input modalities and also has been used to develop a cursor adaptation algorithm to reduce pointing time. Researchers already worked on algorithms to reduce pointing time through determining the difficulty of a task using Fitts' Law [18], increasing target size [5, 22, 27, 34], employing larger cursor activation regions, moving targets closer to cursor location, dragging cursor to nearest target, changing CD ratio [44], and so on. It is certain that these algorithms will perform even better in the existence of a target prediction algorithm so that only correct or most probable targets could be dynamically altered. With this in mind, researchers proposed target or end-point prediction methods.

One of the first algorithms for target prediction was suggested by Murata [36], which calculates the angle deviation towards all possible targets and selects the target with minimum deviation. The results showed that pointing time can be reduced by 25 % using this algorithm [36]. Asano et al. [3] pointed out that having more than one target on a particular movement direction results in poor performances of Murata's algorithm, especially when dealing with targets located far away. They used previous research results about kinematics of pointing tasks and showed that peak velocity and target distance has a linear relationship. They predicted the endpoint through linear regression involving peak velocity and the total distance to endpoint [3]. Lank et al. [29, 38] also employed motion kinematics where they assume minimum jerk law for pointing motion and fit a quadratic function to partial trajectory to predict endpoint. Ziebart et al. [49] used inverse optimal control equations to predict target and compared its performance with other polynomial equations modeling cursor trajectory.

Target prediction algorithms will really be beneficial where people may find a regular pointing device difficult to use. Two possible scenarios are users with motor impairment and first time users for a novel interaction device. There is a plethora of studies demonstrating difficulty of people with age-related or physical impairment in stopping pointer movements or clicking on small target. Cursor movements vary in characteristics for motor-impaired users since they experience tremor, muscular spasms and weakness [23, 26, 37]. The velocity profile includes several stops and jerky movements. This needs to be taken into account when applying target prediction. State space filtering techniques [31], in particular particle filters [20] are found to be promising [28] in estimating intended targets as well as smoothing cursor trajectories.

Another possible scenario is using novel interaction device involving head or eye-gaze movement. Devices like head or eye-gaze trackers are not as easily controllable as a desktop mouse or touchpad and people may struggle to use these devices to precisely control pointing movement. Devices like head or eye-gaze trackers have immense applications for both physical and situational impairment (e.g. operating Alternative and Augmentative Communication software by disabled users using eye-gaze tracker and locking a target by fighter aircraft pilots using head tracker).

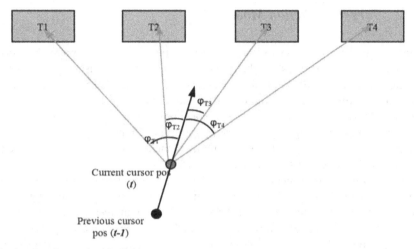

Fig. 3.1 Bearing angle calculation

However, there are not much reported work on target prediction for motor-impaired users except Godsill's work [28] on particle filter and Wobbrock's work [44] on Angle Mouse. There are also almost no attempt to use target prediction algorithms for novel interaction devices like eye-gaze, gesture or head tracking systems. This chapter reports three user studies, where we used a neural network-based target prediction system for elderly users using a computer mouse and able-bodied users using a head tracker involving brain computer interface (BCI) and an eye-gaze tracking based system.

3.2 Theory

3.2.1 Feature Calculation

We have used the following features as input to our models for target prediction. This section explains the features in detail.

- **Velocity**: We have recorded the pointer position using the getCurrentPosition() API, which records pointer position in every 15 ms. The velocity is measured as the ratio of the Euclidian distance between two consecutive readings to the difference in timestamp in milliseconds.
- **Acceleration**: The ratio of two consecutive velocity readings to the time difference between them in milliseconds.
- **Bearing Angle**: This is calculated as the angle between two vectors (Fig. 3.1)— first being the previous cursor position to current cursor position and the other one is the current cursor position to target position.

3.2.2   Target Prediction Model

Pointing tasks are traditionally modeled as a rapid aiming movement. In 1887, Woodsworth [45] first proposed the idea of existence of two phases of movements in a rapid aiming movement, main movement and homing phase, which was later formulated to predict pointing time by Paul Fitts. The study of Fitts' law [18] has been widely used in computer science to model pointing movement in a direct manipulation interface though its applicability for users with motor impairment is still debatable. However, the existence of main movement and homing phase is generally accepted among all users' groups [8, 23, 26].

Once a pointing movement is in homing phase, we can assume the user is pretty near to his intended target. The present algorithm tries to identify the homing phase and then predict the intended target. Previous work on analysing cursor traces of users with a wide range of abilities concentrated on angle [44], velocity and acceleration profiles [23]. So we consider velocity, angle and acceleration of movement and with the help of a back-propagation neural network, try to identify the homing phase.

We used the simplest model available that can classify a dataset non-linearly. Neural network is a mathematical model containing interconnected nodes (or neurons) inspired by biological neurons used as a classifier and pattern recognizer for complex data set. Before using this model, we tried to fit different functions to predict homing phase from velocity, acceleration and bearing angle using two different curve-fitting software and found higher-order polynomial equations worked in most cases though having different coefficients for different devices and users. So we used a model that can automatically learn new polynomial equations. The neural network model was trained using the standard backpropagation algorithm, which was coded by authors. Even after prior training, the neural network keeps training itself during interaction. As a user undertakes a pointing task, the model trains itself. If the user hovers on the target area without clicking, it trains itself for homing phase; otherwise it trains itself for the main movement. At the same time the model is run to get prediction. If it predicts a homing phase, we change colour or enlarge the target.

We have used a three-layer backpropagation network for this study. After the neural network predicts the homing phase, we predict the nearest target from current location towards the direction of movement as the intended target. A simple version of the algorithm is as follows:

For every change in position of pointer on screen

Calculate angle of the movement
Calculate velocity of the movement
Calculate acceleration of the movement

Run neural network with angle, velocity and acceleration

Check output

If output predicts in homing phase
    Find direction of the movement
    Find the nearest target from current location towards the direction of movement

3.2.3   Eye-Gaze Tracker

We used a Tobii X120 eye tracker [40] and the Tobii software development kit (SDK) is used to read raw coordinates of eye-gaze movement. Eye movement is different from a mouse movement as it does not smoothly move in a continuous space as a mouse. The eye-gaze rather follows a spotlight metaphor, and the saccade focuses at the regions of interest. The raw reading from the eye tracker results in jerky movement of the pointer in the screen and it never stays steady at a single location, which makes it difficult to make a selection. We record the eye-gaze positions continuously and average the pixel locations in every 400 ms to estimate the region of interest or saccadic focus points. We simulate the eye movement using a Beizer curve [39] that smoothes the cursor movement between two focus points. We push the focus points into a stack, and the Beizer curve algorithm interpolates points between two focus points. The user needs to blink his eyes to make a selection. The system can classify between intentional and non-intentional eye blinks and only recognizes the intentional ones through dwell time adjustment.

3.2.4   Head Tracker

The head tracking was conducted using an Emotiv Epoch BCI Headset [14]. The headset has an internal gyroscope that can detect head movement. The Emotiv SDK was used to extract raw coordinates from head movement and a Beizer curve [39] was used to smooth cursor movement on screen. We used an eye-blink to make a selection. The Emotiv Headset [14] can detect a blink from electroencephalography (EEG) measurement without any prior training of participants. We developed software that smoothes up the cursor movement following head movement and make a mouse click if the user blinks his eyes.

Section 3.6 presents a detailed literature survey on existing head and eye tracking research with an emphasis on multimodal head and eye tracking systems.

3.3   Evaluation Criteria

Once we have a working algorithm that can predict intended target, we need to evaluate its performance so that we can compare and contrast its performance with prior research. So far there is not much consensus on the evaluation criteria for target prediction algorithms. We have defined the following three parameters to evaluate the quality of a target prediction algorithm.

Availability In how many pointing tasks the algorithm makes a successful prediction.

For example, a user has undertaken ten pointing tasks. An algorithm that correctly predicts target in seven of them is better than another one, which is successful in predicting correct target in five pointing tasks.

Accuracy Percentage of correct prediction among all predictions.

Any target recognition algorithm keeps on predicting target, while the user is moving a pointer in a screen. It may happen that within a single pointing task, an algorithm initially predicts a wrong target, but as the user gets closer to the intended target, the algorithm finds the correct target. So if an algorithm predicts an intended target 100 times among which 70 are correct, its accuracy will be 70%.

This metric complements the previous metric. For example, we have an algorithm that predicts the nearest target from the current pointer location as the intended target. This algorithm will have 100% availability as it will fire in all pointing tasks but with pretty low accuracy, while there are multiple targets available on the path of pointer.

Sensitivity How quickly an algorithm can detect intended target.

For example, an algorithm that can find the intended target, while the user crossed 90% of target distance or pointing time is less sensitive than an algorithm that can predict correct target after the user crosses only 70% of target distance or pointing time.

3.4   Implementation and Validation

We have implemented a bank of neural networks considering all possible combinations of three movement properties (bearing, velocity and acceleration of movement). We have used supervised learning to detect users' movement phases from movement features. Initially, we trained the neural networks with a multiple distractor task. Later we used the same task to evaluate the networks following our evaluation criteria. Our training and test set of participants were different.

We conducted three user trials involving three different input modalities:

1. The first trial involved people with age-related and physical impairment and they used a standard computer mouse.
2. The second trial involved a head tracker and BCI used by able-bodied users who never used similar system before.
3. The third trial involved an eye-gaze tracker used by able-bodied users who never used similar system before.

We described these trials in the following sections. Besides the target prediction system we also present an analysis of cursor trajectories for the head and eye-gaze tracking systems.

3.4.1   Participants

We have collected data from 23 users using mouse. The users used to operate computer everyday and volunteered for the study. The group of participants included users with a wide range of abilities in terms of visual and motor impairment. Age-related impaired users were more than 60 years old and physically impaired users suffer from cerebral palsy or spinabifida.

We trained the neural networks with 13 users among which five have age-related or physical impairment (like cerebral palsy). Then we test the system with ten participants among which five have age-related visual and motor impairment. The gender was balanced to nearly 1:1 in both training and test cases.

The head tracking system was evaluated by eight able-bodied users (five males, three females) aged between 20 and 35. They never used any head tracking system before.

The eye tracking system was evaluated by eight able-bodied users (five males, three females) aged between 20 and 45. They never used the eye tracking system before. They did not have any trouble in using the experimental set-up.

These studies were conducted at Cambridge, UK.

3.4.2   Material

The study was conducted using a 21-inch screen (435×325 mm) with 1600×1200 pixels resolution and a standard computer mouse. The head tracking was conducted by using Emotiv Epoch BCI headset [18], while a Tobii X120 eye tracker is used for eye tracking.

3.4.3   Procedure

The task was like the ISO 9241 pointing task with multiple distractors on screen (Fig. 3.2). We tried to strike a balance between the complete natural interaction scenario of Input Observer system [15] and the controlled single target task [18, 32] of traditional Fitts' Law analysis. We developed software to conduct this task, which automatically records mouse locations and events on the screen in every 16 ms.

Users need to click the button at the centre of the screen and then the target button appears with other distractors. We used five different target sizes (20, 40, 30, 50, 60 pixels) and source to target distances (100, 140, 180, 240, 300 pixels). The participants using mouse were instructed to click target for 10 min after they were briefed about the procedure.

For the head tracking based system, we used five different target sizes (40, 50, 60, 70, 80 pixels) and source to target distances (100, 160, 220, 280, 350 pixels). The participants were instructed to click target for 5 min after they were briefed about the procedure.

Fig. 3.2 Multiple distractor task

We calibrated the eye tracking system with nine dots before start of trial with each participant. The system was kept on calibrating until the Tobii SDK did not need any further recalibration. Users need to click the button at the centre of the screen and then the target button appears with other distractors. We used five different target sizes (60, 70, 80, 90, 100 pixels) and source to target distances (160, 220, 280, 350, 400 pixels). We have to change the target size and amplitude than the head tracking system as it was too difficult even for the developer to select target less than 60 pixels wide using the eye tracking system. The participants were instructed to click target for 5 min after calibration.

3.4.4   Results

3.4.4.1   Target Prediction Analysis

Figures 3.3 and 3.4 plot the average percentage of availability and accuracy in different systems. In Figs. 3.3 and 3.4, different combinations of features are plotted in X-axis, while the average availability and accuracy is plotted in Y-axis. The model only fires (or turns available) when it detects a change in movement phase. In certain occasions, it fails to detect this change of movement phases, and so, the availability is not always 100%. In Fig. 3.3, the green (or the first) bar shows the percentage of correct prediction and the red (or the second) bar shows the percentage of wrong prediction. The white (or the third) bar shows the percentage when the model failed to fire.

Figure 3.5 plots the sensitivity of the system. The X-axis shows the fraction of pointing time spent in a scale of 100. The Y-axis represents the probability of correct target prediction. We found that velocity and bearing of movements have the highest availability for mouse and eye-gaze tracking system, while the combination of all parameters have the highest availability of head tracking system. Velocity and bearing also have the highest accuracy for all systems. The sensitivity is found to be rather same for all possible combinations of parameters.

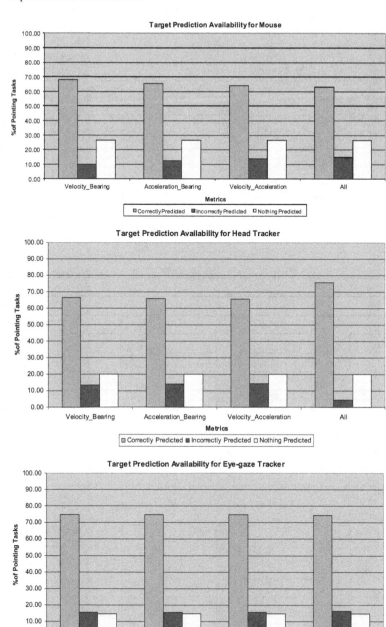

Fig. 3.3 Availability of different systems

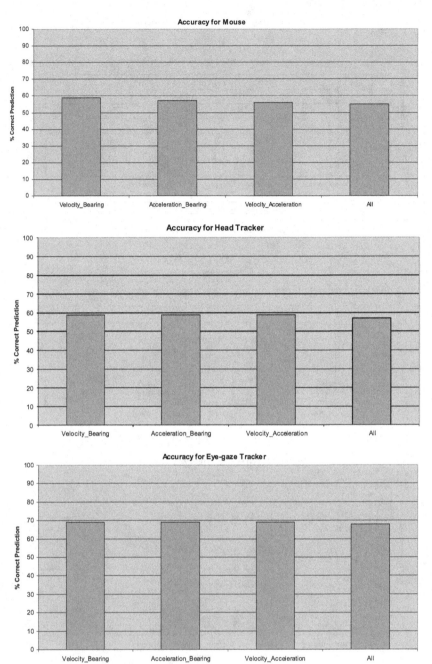

Fig. 3.4 Accuracy of different systems

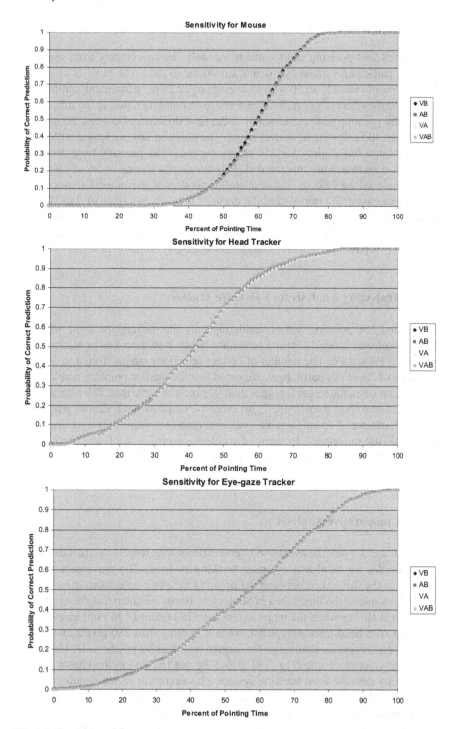

Fig. 3.5 Sensitivity of the system

3.4.4.2   Trajectory Analysis for Head Tracker

We recorded 280 pointing tasks considering only the movements from origin to target and participants made two wrong selections in total. The number of correct selections ranges from 17 to 50 with an average of 28.25 per participant. Initially, we investigated the effect of target distance and size on pointing times. In the subsequent analysis, the pointing time is measured as the time difference between the onset of target screen and selection of correct target. The pointing time increased with target distance though fell slightly for 350 pixels distance. The pointing time decreases as target size increases but increased slightly for targets having width of 80 pixels. We also analysed the velocity and acceleration profiles of movements across screen for each participant. We normalized the distance to target in a scale of 0 to 100 and plotted the instantaneous velocity and acceleration. The velocity profiles had similar inverted U-shape for most participants though the acceleration profiles were quite different for different participants and did not share any common pattern.

3.4.4.3   Trajectory Analysis for Eye-Gaze Tracker

We recorded 180 pointing tasks considering only the movements from origin to target. Participants made 14 wrong selections, while 8 of them can be attributed to participants P2 and P6. The number of correct selections ranges from 8 to 31 with an average of 20.63 per participant. We noted that the median pointing time did not change much when the target is bigger than 80 pixels or more than 280 pixels away. We found that except participant 7, all other participants have similar pattern of velocity. Participant 7 found to make small movements towards the target instead of one big ballistic movement. In terms of acceleration profile, we found participants P3, P6 and P7 have different profiles in terms of sudden hike in acceleration than the rest.

3.4.4.4   Comparative Analysis

Figures 3.6 and 3.7 plot the average movement times with respect to target distances and amplitudes for head and eye-gaze tracking systems. The movement time is measured as the difference between the pointing time and time taken to select the target, which means the time taken to blink eyes. It may be noted that the eye tracking system is slower when the target is less than 280 pixels (≈ 76 mm) away, but it catches up with head tracking system, when it is more than 280 pixels away. The head tracking system is also faster for targets less than 80 pixels wide. However, the average velocity profile (Fig. 3.8) shows the eye tracking system has a greater peak velocity than the head tracking system. The amplitude of acceleration was in the range of 10^{-5} pixel/ms^2 in both cases. However there were distinctive patterns, some users accelerated and decelerated regularly throughout their movement phases, while some had a sudden hike and subsequent drop in acceleration while they

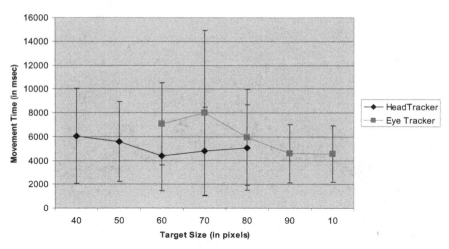

Fig. 3.6. Comparing average movement times with respect to target size

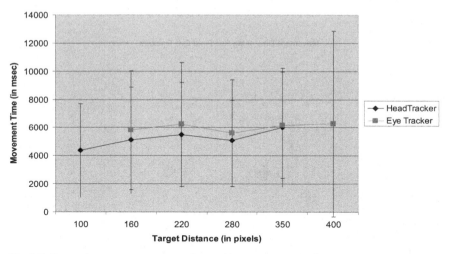

Fig. 3.7 Comparing average movement times with respect to target distance

were within the last 20% of overall target distance. Finally, we plotted the movement time with respect to index of difficulty ($ID = \log_2 \dfrac{D}{W}$, Fig. 3.9). It should be noted here that the ID is just used as a function related to the target distance and the amplitude and may not signify the meaning in terms of Fitts' Law analysis as we do not have enough trial data to apply Fitts' Law. The head tracking system is

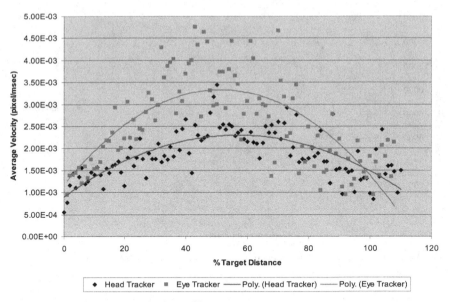

Fig. 3.8 Comparing average velocity profiles

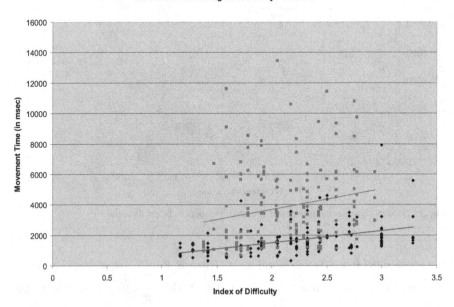

Fig. 3.9 Comparing average pointing times with respect to ID

found significantly faster ($t = 1.97$, $p < 0.001$, two-tailed unequal variance) than the eye tracking system.

Video demonstrations of the multiple distractor task is available at http://youtu.be/QsxDxcccwAw and target prediction system is available at http://youtu.be/p9YOKj59TiY.

3.4.5 Discussion

This study proposes a new model for target prediction based on neural network, and this model has been applied in two different scenarios. The model accurately detects change in pointing phase in more than 70% of the pointing tasks for head and eye-gaze trackers and 65% for mouse used by people with age-related or physical impairment. The accuracy of target prediction is nearly 60% for all cases; however, it reaches more than 90% as the user reaches near the target as shown in the sensitivity graph (Fig. 3.5). We highlight the main contribution of this work in the following sections:

New Model This chapter proposes a new type of model based on Backpropagation Neural Network,, which is better than previous results [29, 49]. For example, Ziebart's models [49] achieve more than 50% accuracy after crossing 70% of pointing time while our models have more than 70% accuracy at similar stage. Furthermore, lack of evaluation metrics makes it difficult to compare different methods in target prediction and most models do not publish results in as much detail as ours. Additionally, most research on target prediction did not include users with age-related or physical impairment.

New Modality of Interaction Previous work on target or end-point prediction did not investigate novel modality of interaction. This work shows that the neural network-based model can also be used for target prediction using the head tracker and BCI based system.

It may be noted that we got the highest accuracy for the eye-gaze tracking based system. The sensitivity pattern is also different for eye-gaze and head tracking systems than mouse. One possible explanation is that the users spent more time in homing phase in head and eye-gaze tracking based systems than mouse. The neural network worked more precisely in the homing phase indicating an adaptation algorithm based on this target prediction model that can significantly reduce time spent in homing phase and the overall pointing time as well.

However, one disadvantage of our model is we need to know the target locations to find the correct target. Research on interface layout description languages like UIML will be useful in this context. Dixon's [10] work on target identification and his implementation of Bubble Cursor [34] will be a good complement for this target prediction system.

Evaluation Metrics This chapter proposes a set of metrics to evaluate target prediction algorithms and compare their performance for different applications. An application developer may choose an appropriate model or algorithm based on these evaluation metrics.

For example, if an interface has closely spaced small icons like a toolbar or menu, we should prefer an algorithm with high accuracy, perhaps compromising availability. However, for large screen display or pointing through gesture, we should prefer an algorithm with high availability as otherwise users may not feel any effect of target prediction. Choice of an algorithm also depends on the effect of target prediction algorithms. For example, after predicting a target, we may simply highlight the target or proactively move the cursor on the button. In the first case, an algorithm with high availability is good as users can always get a feedback based on their movement. However, in case of proactive cursor movement based on target prediction, we should choose an algorithm with high accuracy, otherwise a wrong prediction will frustrate users and in fact may increase pointing time.

Best Set of Features We found that in case of neural network model, a model based on velocity and bearing of movement worked best. Future researchers can exploit this information to propose new models and algorithms.

Head and Eye-Gaze Tracking Based Systems As part of this study, we also developed smoothing algorithms for head and eye-gaze tracking based systems. All participants could use the head and eye-gaze tracking systems with the help of our smoothing algorithms within the 5 min trial duration without any prior training. Their main difficulty was at home on small target, especially with the eye-gaze tracking based system. Our study also points out the minimum target size and the distance required for each interface and estimates of pointing times for first time users, which may be useful for developing eye-gaze or head tracking based applications. The comparative analysis can also help to develop input devices combining both head and eye-gaze trackers.

3.5 Adaptive System

The main purpose of developing the target prediction system is to reduce pointing times. After validating the target prediction model, we tested its performance again as an adaptation algorithm. We have developed an adaptation system that enlarges a target, whenever it is predicted as a probable target. Recent work by Hwang [22] already found similar technique can reduce pointing times for older adults in a single target task though Lee [30] did not find a significant reduction of pointing times in multiple distractor task.

We used the similar multiple distractor set up as our previous studies described above. In this study, whenever the target prediction system predicts a target, we increased its size by 1.5 times. We do not change the colour or any other property of the target. We have evaluated this adaptation system with the head tracker system.

3.5.1   *Participants*

We have evaluated this adaptation system by six able-bodied users (four males, two females) with an age range between 22 and 45.

3.5.2   *Material*

We used the same screen and head tracker hardware and software for this study.

3.5.3   *Procedure*

It was same as the multiple distractor task described above, participants were not trained with the adaptation system before the trial and they were using it for the first time.

3.5.4   *Results*

We recorded 181 pointing tasks and there were five instances of wrong selection. A *SIZE* × *ADAPTATION* ANOVA on pointing time found a significant effect of adaptation (F (1,27)=31.53, $p<0.01$, $\eta^2=0.54$) while a *DISTANCE* × *ADAPTATION* ANOVA also found a significant effect of adaptation (F (1,31)=30.05, $p<0.01$, $\eta^2=0.49$). Figures 3.10 and 3.11 show the average pointing time for different target sizes and distances in adapted and non-adapted versions.

3.5.5   *Discussion*

This study shows that the target prediction system can reduce pointing time when coupled with a target magnification system. Although this study only evaluated head tracker, but future work will include other modalities of interaction. It can be noted that the differences between adapted and non-adapted pointing times increase for smaller targets and longer source to target distances. We can assume that presence of such target prediction and adaptation system will not only reduce pointing times for existing eye-gaze and head tracking interfaces but also allow better utilization of screen space as target sizes can be reduced and more targets can be used in a single screen.

This system will be particularly useful for information visualization and assistive interfaces. For example, certain part of a graph or an image thumbnail among a set of other images can be zoomed in by detecting users' intended target. In existing

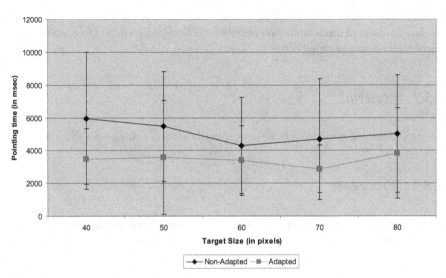

Fig. 3.10 Adaptation system with respect to target size

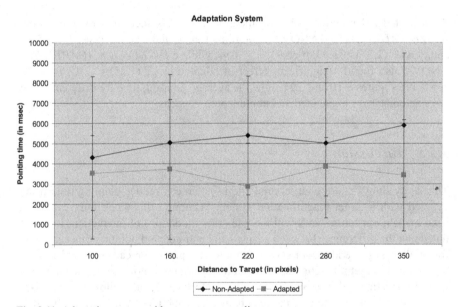

Fig. 3.11 Adaptation system with respect to target distance

image search interfaces at Google Chrome or Internet Explorer, an image is only zoomed in after the user clicks on it, while using the present system any thumbnail can be zoomed in without needing an explicit selection by user. This automatic zooming will be useful for image analysis (e.g. disease analysis from image of crops, analysis of CCTV image during a disaster etc). This technique will also be useful in assistive interfaces, where the zooming level of the screen magnifier can be adjusted based on the output from the target prediction model.

3.6 Related Work

There is a plethora of studies on inventing and comparing new modalities of interaction. Most of these studies conduct a pointing and clicking or dragging task in a screen and report the index of performance of the new input device according to Fitts' Law. For example, MacKenzie, Sellen and Buxton [32] compared mouse, stylus and trackball, while Jagacinski and Monk [25] compared helmet-mounted sight and joystick. In recent time, Vertegaal [41] conducted similar studies with mouse, stylus and eye-gaze tracker. Ware et al. [43] and Miniotas [35] also conducted similar Fitts' law [18] analysis for eye-gaze tracker. Though these studies found mouse or stylus are faster than trackball, head or eye-gaze tracker, but still there are certain cases of physical and situational impairment, those require the use of these devices [2]. Additionally, with advent of computer vision and infrared trackers, eye-gaze and head trackers are turning cheaper and portable finding their use in everyday products like tablets and smart-phones.

Research on eye tracking dated back to late eighteenth century when Louis Émile Javal investigated saccadic movements in a reading task [21]. Edmund Huey pioneered in building the first eye tracker, which was a contact lens connected with an aluminum pointer [21]. At present time, eye tracking research [13, 33] can be classified according to the following diagram (Fig. 3.12).

Research on developing eye tracker investigates on reducing the cost of existing infra-red based trackers (e.g. Tobii [40] or FaceLab [16] Tracker) as well as increasing their accuracy. Researchers also worked on developing customized eye trackers for tasks that do not require precise x and y coordinates as input from the tracker [12, 48]. On a different set of applications, eye trackers often help to design better billboards, traffic signs and advertising posters through analysis of users' eye-gaze patterns [11, 13, 33]. This analysis even leads to developing models to simulate eye-gaze movements including people with various visual impairments [6]. Eye trackers can also be used as an interaction device to control electronic devices and applications [1, 8, 42]. This role of eye trackers becomes more significant for certain types of users with physical impairment [1, 42] (e.g. ALS, severe spasticity, cerebral palsy and so on) and situation impairment (e.g. aircraft pilot operating under high G-force).

Zhai [47] and Jacob [24] presented a detailed list of advantages and disadvantages of using eye–gaze-based pointing devices. Researchers already attempted to

Fig. 3.12 Taxonomy of eye tracking research

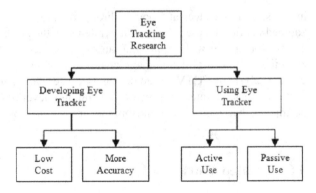

couple other modalities of interaction with eye-gaze tracking to solve the 'Midas-Touch' or selection problem. Existing eye tracking systems make a selection through dwell time adjustment or eye blinks. Zhai's MAGIC system [47] took an innovative step towards multimodal eye tracking system through using a different modality for selecting target. Recent research has also tried to combine other assistive technology like single-switch scanning system with eye tracking system [7]. Ashdown et al. [4] addressed the issue of head movement while tracking eye-gaze in a multiple monitor scenario. They used head tracking to switch pointer across screens, which was preferred by participants, but in effect increased pointing time. Dostal et al. [12] addressed similar issues by detecting which monitor the user is looking at through analysing webcam video. The SideWays system [48] does not need personalized calibration and can scroll contents of a display screen by detecting eye-gaze. The system identifies whether users are looking at the middle or sides of a display and if they are looking to the sides, the system scrolls content at the middle. Both Dostal's system and SideWays system do not use precise x and y coordinates to move a mouse pointer. Fu and Huang [19] proposed an input system hMouse, which moves a pointer based on head movement. They detected head movement by analysing video input and their system is found to outperform another similar system called CameraMouse [9]. Fejtova's Magic Key system [17] also uses a webcam like CameraMouse [9] but the pointer is moved on the screen based on the position of nose (nostrils to be precise). Selection is done by eye blinks. Bates [5] multimodal eye tracking system allows zooming portion of screen using a polhemus tracker. Zandera et al. [46] combine a BCI system with eye-gaze tracking, where EEG generated by imagining a rinsing action is trained to make a selection. However, their system had limited success in reducing pointing times. Our future work will combine the eye-gaze tracker, head tracker and BCI system into a single multimodal unit, while the target prediction model will be used to adapt interaction. Our present study shows that the combined system along with the target prediction model has the potential to significantly reduce pointing times.

3.7 Conclusions

This chapter proposes a framework to evaluate target prediction algorithms and then proposes an algorithm based on a neural network-based model. We compared the performance of the algorithm for people with a wide range of abilities and three different input modalities and obtained more than 60 % accuracy of prediction in all cases. Finally, we combined the target prediction system with a target magnification algorithm that statistically significantly reduced pointing times. As part of the study, we also described smoothing algorithms for an eye-gaze tracker and presented a comparative analysis of cursor trajectories of eye-gaze and head tracking systems.

References

1. Adjouadi, M., Sesin, A., Ayala, M., & Cabrerizo, M. (2004). Remote eye gaze tracking system as a computer interface for persons with severe motor disability. *ICCHP 2004, LNCS, 3118*, 761–769.
2. Allison, R. S., Eizenman, M., & Cheung, B. S. K. (1996). Combined head and eye tracking system for dynamic testing of the vestibular system. *IEEE Transaction on Biomedical Engineering, 43*(11).
3. Asano, T., Sharlin, E., Kitamura, Y., Takashima, K., & Kishino, F. (2005). *Predictive interaction using the delphian desktop*. Proceedings of the 186th annual ACM smposium on User Interface Software and Technology (UIST 2005) (pp. 133–141), New York.
4. Ashdown, M., Oka, K., & Sato, Y. (2005). *Combining head tracking and mouse input for a GUI on multiple monitors*. CHI Late breaking Result.
5. Bates, R. (1999). *Multimodal eye-based interaction for zoomed target selection on a standard graphical user interface*. INTERACT.
6. Biswas, P., & Robinson, P. (2009). *Modelling perception using image processing algorithms*. 23rd British computer society conference on Human-Computer Interaction (HCI 2009)
7. Biswas, P., & Langdon, P. (June 2011). A new input system for disabled users involving eye gaze tracker and scanning interface. *Journal of Assistive Technologies, 5*(2). ISSN:1754-9450
8. Biswas, P., & Langdon, P. (2012). Developing multimodal adaptation algorithm for mobility impaired users by evaluating their hand strength. *International Journal of Human-Computer Interaction, 28*(9). (Taylor & Francis, Print ISSN:1044-7318).
9. CameraMouse. (2013). http://www.cameramouse.com. Accessed 22 Sep 2013.
10. Dixon, M., Fogarty, J., & Wobbrock, J. (2012). *A general-purpose target-aware pointing enhancement using pixel-level analysis of graphical interfaces*. Proceedings of the 2012 ACM Annual Conference on Human Factors in Computing Systems (CHI 2012) (pp. 3167–3176). New York: ACM.
11. Donegan, M., et al. (2009). Understanding users and their needs. *Universal Access in the Information Society, 8*, 259–275.
12. Dostal, J., Kristensson, P. O., & Quigley, A. (2013). *Subtle gaze-dependent techniques for visualising display changes in multi-display environments*. ACM international conference of Intelligent User Interfaces (IUI 2013).
13. Duchowski, A. T. (2007). *Eye tracking methodology*. New York: Springer.
14. Emotiv Epoch (2013). http://www.emotiv.com/. Accessed 31 Aug 2013.
15. Evans, A. C., & Wobbrock, J. O. (5–10 May 2012). *Taming wild behavior: The input observer for obtaining text entry and mouse pointing measures from everyday computer use*. Proceedings of the ACM conference on Human Factors in Computing Systems (CHI '12). Austin, Texas (pp. 1947–1956). New York: ACM.

16. Facelab Eye Tracker (2013). http://www.seeingmachines.com/product/facelab/. Accessed 29 April 2013.
17. Fejtova, M., et al. (2009). Hands-free interaction with a computer and other technologies. *Universal Access in the Information Society, 8.*
18. Fitts, P. M. (1954). The information capacity of the human motor system in controlling the amplitude of movement. *Journal of Experimental Psychology, 47,* 381–391.
19. Fu, Y., & Huang, T. S. (2007). *hMouse: Head tracking driven virtual computer mouse.* IEEE workshop on applications of computer vision.
20. Godsill, S., & Vermaak, J. (2004). Models and algorithms for tracking using variable dimension particle filters. *International conference on acoustics, speech and signal processing.*
21. Huey, E. (1908). *The psychology and pedagogy of reading.* Cambridge: MIT Press.
22. Hwang, F., Hollinworth, N., & Williams, N. (2013). ACM Transactions on Accessible Computing (TACCESS) 5(1).
23. Hwang, F., Keates, S., Langdon, P., & Clarkson, P. J. (2005). A submovement analysis of cursor trajectories. *Behaviour and Information Technology, 24*(3), 205–217.
24. Jacob, R. (1993). Eye movement-based human-computer interaction techniques: Toward non-command interfaces. *Advances in Human-Computer Interaction.*
25. Jagacinski, R. J., & Monk, D. L. (1985). Fitts' Law in two dimensions with hand and head movements. *Journal of Motor Behaviour, 17*(1), 77–95.
26. Keates, S., Hwang, F., Langdon, P., Clarkson, P. J., & Robinson, P. (2002). Cursor measures for motion-impaired computer users. *Proceedings of the fifth international ACM conference on Assistive Technologies—ASSETS* (pp. 135–142). New York
27. Lane, D. M., Peres, S. C., Sándor, A., & Napier, H. A. (2005). A process for anticipating and executing icon selection in graphical user interfaces. *International Journal of Human Computer Interaction, 19*(2), 243–254.
28. Langdon, P. M., Godsill, S., & Clarkson, P. J. (2006). Statistical estimation of user's interactions from motion impaired cursor use data. *6th International Conference on Disability, Virtual Reality and Associated Technologies (ICDVRAT 2006)*, Esbjerg.
29. Lank, E., Cheng, Y. N., & Ruiz, J. (2007). Endpoint prediction using motion kinematics. *Proceedings of the SIGCHI conference on Human factors in computing systems (CHI '07)* (pp. 637–646). New York.
30. Lee, D., Kwon, S., & Chung, M. K. (2012). Effects of user age and target-expansion methods on target-acquisition tasks using a mouse. *Applied Ergonomics, 43*(1), 166–175.
31. Li, X. R., & Jilkov, V. P. (2003). Survey of maneuvering target tracking. Part I. Dynamic models. *IEEE Transactions on Aerospace and Electronic Systems, 39*(4), 1333–1364.
32. MacKenzie, I. S., Sellen, A., & Buxton, W. (1991). *A comparison of input devices in elemental pointing and dragging tasks.* Proceedings of the CHI '91 conference on Human factors in computing systems (pp. 161–166). New York: ACM.
33. Majaranta, P., & Raiha, K. (2002) *Twenty years of eye typing: Systems and design issues.* Eye tracking research & application.
34. McGuffin, M. J., & Balakrishnan, R. (2005). Fitts' law and expanding targets: Experimental studies and designs for user interfaces. *ACM Transactions Computer-Human Interaction, 12*(4), 388–422.
35. Miniotas, D. (2001). *Application of Fitts' Law to eye gaze interaction.* Proceedings of the ACM SIGCHI conference on Human factors in computing systems (CHI) (pp. 339–340).
36. Murata, A. (1998). Improvement of pointing time by predicting targets in pointing with a PC mouse. *International Journal of Human-Computer Interaction, 10*(1), 23–32.
37. Oirschot, H., & Houtsma, A. J. M. (2001) Cursor trajectory analysis. In S. Brewster & R. Murray-Smith (Eds.), *Haptic Human-Computer Interaction* (LNCS Vol. 2058, pp. 127–134). Springer: Berlin.
38. Ruiz, J., & Lank, E. (2010). *Speeding pointing in tiled widgets: Understanding the effects of target expansion and misprediction.* Proceedings of the 15th international conference on Intelligent User Interfaces (IUI'10) (pp. 229–238). New York: ACM.

39. Salomon, D. (Aug. 2005). *Curves and surfaces for computer graphics* (ISBN:0-387-24196-24195). New York: Springer.
40. Tobii X120 Eye Tracker. (2013). http://www.tobii.com/en/eye-tracking-research/global/products/hardware/tobii-x60x120-eye-tracker/. Accessed 31 Aug 2013.
41. Vertegaal, R. (2008). *A Fitts' Law comparison of eye tracking and manual input in the selection of visual targets*. Proceedings of the international conference of multimodal interaction (pp. 241–248).
42. Ward, D. (2010). Dasher with an eye-tracker. http://www.inference.phy.cam.ac.uk/djw30/dasher/eye.html. Accessed 19 Aug 2010.
43. Ware, C., & Mikaelian, H. M. (1987). *An evaluation of an eye tracker as a device for computer input*. Proceedings of the ACM SIGCHI conference on Human factors in computing systems (CHI) (pp. 183–187).
44. Wobbrock, J. O., Fogarty, J., Liu, S., Kimuro, S., & Harada, S. (2009). *The angle mouse: Target-agnostic dynamic gain adjustment based on angular deviation*. Proceedings of the 27th international conference on Human factors in computing systems (CHI '09) (pp. 1401–1410). New York.
45. Woodworth, R. S. (1899). The accuracy of voluntary movement. *Psychological Review, 3*, 1–119.
46. Zandera, T. O., Gaertnera, M., Kothea, C., & Vilimek, R. (2010). Combining eye gaze input with a brain-computer interface for touchless human-computer interaction. *International Journal of Human-Computer Interaction, 27*(1).
47. Zhai, S., Morimoto, C., & Ihde, S. (1999). *Manual and Gaze Input Cascaded (MAGIC) Pointing*. ACM SIGCHI conference on Human factors in computing system (CHI).
48. Zhang, Y., Bulling, A., & Gellersen, H. (2013). *SideWays: A gaze interface for spontaneous interaction with situated displays*. CHI 2013.
49. Ziebart, B., Dey, A., & Bagnell, J. A. (2012). *Probabilistic pointing target prediction via inverse optimal control*. Proceedings of the 2012 ACM international conference on Intelligent User Interfaces (IUI '12) (pp. 1–10). New York.

Chapter 4
New Interfaces

Charity (and experiment) begins at home - author's mother testing the eye tracking
based shopping application

4.1 Introduction

Chapter 2 has discussed about personalizing existing (or third-party) interfaces,
while Chap. 3 introduced new modalities of interaction and a target prediction
technology. This chapter proposes a new set of interfaces for everyday computing
tasks like electronic shopping, banking, travelling and so on. Unlike the weather
monitoring and electronic agriculture systems, here we do not propose a whole new
application, rather we emphasize only on the interfaces and interaction.

P. Biswas, *Inclusive Human Machine Interaction for India,*
Human–Computer Interaction Series, DOI 10.1007/978-3-319-06500-7_4,
© Springer International Publishing Switzerland 2014

We have initially developed a design bed incorporating the target prediction technology discussed in the previous chapter. The design bed uses 18-point font size and big buttons to facilitate interaction by people with age-related impairment. Each interface tries to reduce information overload by providing only minimum required details. Users do not need to precisely point on target, the target prediction technology automatically sets focus on a button when a pointer reaches near it. The (gray in B&W) buttons in Fig. 4.1 depict these predicted targets. However, the button is not selected automatically, the user needs to give a second input in terms of a keypress, mouse click, or blink to make the final selection.

This chapter evaluates how Indian users interact with eye-gaze tracking systems. Eye-gaze tracking systems are pretty intuitive to operate and have good potential to be incorporated into mainstream electronic devices. In the Indian context, eye-gaze or head movement tracking system can even replace or augment the standard computer mouse or a TV remote as we found in the survey that many elderly users did not find the computer mouse intuitive or found it difficult to read the labels on a TV remote. The eye-gaze tracking research is advancing rapidly in terms of both reducing price and increasing accuracy of tracking. Indian universities have enough expertise to built customized accurate eye-gaze trackers using infrared LEDs.

In this chapter, we have reported the following three user trials all involving the same eye-gaze tracking system discussed in the previous chapter.

1. The first trial reports interactions with the weather monitoring system as discussed in Chap. 2.
2. The second trial compares cognitive load and selection time for a standard computer mouse and eye-gaze tracking system for the electronic shopping application
3. The third trial presents a longitudinal study to investigate the effect of learning on eye-gaze tracking based interaction.

It may be noted that both Chap. 3 and this chapter are reporting trials involving eye-gaze tracker. However, the user trials are different in terms of primary and secondary tasks. Users' primary task was only to point and select in trials as reported in the previous chapter, while users performed a different task in trials as reported in this chapter. Their primary tasks were reporting weather or shopping. Pointing and selection were secondary tasks. So studies reported in this chapter are more externally valid or closer to reality than the ones described in Chap. 3.

4.2   User Trial on Weather Monitoring System

This trial used the Wisekar weather monitoring system described in Chap. 2. The aim of the study was to estimate selection times for an application that is not customized for eye-gaze tracking system without using any target prediction algorithm. We recruited participants who were not expert computer users and more than 50 years old. This study served as a control condition for the later studies on the e-shopping application involving the design bed incorporated with the target prediction system.

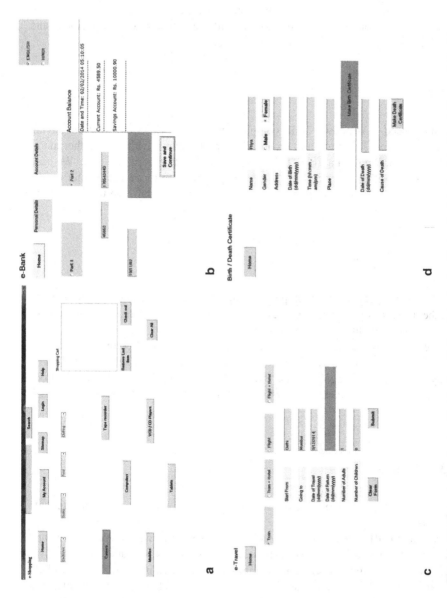

Fig. 4.1 Interfaces designed using the target prediction design bed. **a** Electronic shopping Interface. **b** Electronic Banking Interface. **c** Electronic Travelling Interface. **d** Birth/Death Registration System

4.2.1 Participants

We have collected data from five users (four males, one female, average age 54 years). They are the same set of users described in Sect. 3.1.1 of Chap. 2 except participants P3 and P6. These participants were not expert computer users; they used computers occasionally for specific purposes like emailing, drafting document, and so on. The study was conducted at Delhi, India.

4.2.2 Material

We have used a Windows 7 HP computer with 54 cm × 33 cm monitor having 1920 × 1080 pixels resolution to record users' performance with the weather monitoring system. We used a Tobii Tx2 eye-gaze tracker to record eye-gaze. We used the same algorithm described in the previous chapter to move the pointer on the screen. This study did not use any target prediction algorithm. We used eye-blink to select target.

4.2.3 Procedure

The task was to report latest temperature and humidity of cities using the Wisekar weather monitoring system (Fig. 4.2). Each participant was instructed to report temperature and humidity of any two cities.

They needed to select a bubble with the city name, then click on the 'Weather' menu item at the top of the screen, and then again click on the second bubble with a city name and click again on the 'Weather' menu item. It needed two selections (one on the bubble and another on the 'Weather' menu item) to complete the task one reporting.

4.3 Results

We analyzed the selection times of each user separately and then made an aggregate analysis.

Participant P1 made three successful selections (clicking on two bubbles and once on the 'Weather' menu item). His selection times were 3, 2, and 2 s, respectively. However, during each selection, he made a double click instead of a single click.

Participant P2 made three successful selections (clicking on two bubbles and once on the "Weather" menu item). His selection times were 10, 6, and 10s, respectively. However, after the third selection, he could not make another successful selection within the next 57 s and then gave up.

Participant P4 made four successful selections. His selection times were 4, 9, 46, and 9 s, respectively. During the third selection, he was trying to select the 'DEL'

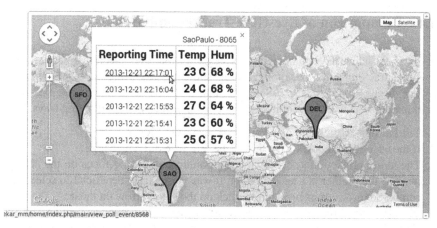

Fig. 4.2 Screenshots of Wisekar weather monitoring system

captioned bubble, but he twice clicked outside the bubble causing the map to zoom out and the recovery process needed to click again on the 'Weather' menu item. The overall error recovery and selection process took 46 s.

Participant P5 made four successful selections. Her selection times were 2, 2, 4, and 49 s, respectively. During the first selection, she made a double click instead of a single click. After the third selection, she took 49 s to select the 'Weather' menu item making several missed clicks outside the target. After the fourth selection, she spent 56 s to click on another city bubble, but could not succeed and finally gave up.

Participant P7 made five successful selections. His selection times were 2, 4, 60, 2, and 2s, respectively. He also struggled to select the 'DEL' captioned bubble like P4, but finally recovered and made two more successful selections.

The average selection time was 12 s considering all selections and was 4.56 s considering the ones without any missed clicks outside the target.

4.3.1 Discussion

This pilot study shows that even first-time users can use an eye-gaze tracking interface for a web browser. However, except P1, all other participants were stuck at least once either due to wrong selection or trying to select a small menu item. Their average time of selection was also too long for practical purposes. The Google Maps interfaces were also not very suitable for eye-gaze tracking based interaction as a missed selection outside the bubble zoomed in the map, often removing the bubble from view. The following two user trials incorporate the target prediction technology discussed in Chap. 3 and also use the e-Shopping interface, which is more suitable for eye tracking based interaction than Google Maps.

4.4 Comparison of Eye-Gaze Tracker and Mouse

In this user trial we have compared users' cognitive load and selection times between eye-gaze tracking and mouse for an online shopping task using the e-Shopping interface discussed above. The e-Shopping interface was more suitable for eye-gaze tracking than the weather monitoring system's interface in the following ways:

1. The buttons or clickable items on the screen were bigger.
2. If the user clicked outside the target, the interface did not change.
3. The target prediction system helped in pointing by setting focus on the screen items if the pointer is near the target. It was particularly beneficial to select the combo boxes, as users need not to click on the small arrow on those.
4. The clickable screen items were well separated to avoid wrong selection.
5. The selection mechanism of eye-gaze tracking system was changed—instead of blinking, users needed to press the spacebar on the keyboard to make a selection.

We collected data from elderly and novice participants and the study aims to find how easy or difficult users perceive and perform with eye-gaze tracking based system in comparison to mouse, which is still now the most commonly used computer input device. Vertegaal [1] already compared eye-gaze tracking and mouse-based interaction for pointing and clicking tasks and found that eye-gaze tracking with dwell time-based selection is faster than the mouse, but eye-gaze tracking also generated higher error rate.

4.4.1 Participants

We collected data from eight users (six males, two females, average age 57 years). All users use a computer but not on a regular basis. They use it for fixed tasks like emailing, drafting document, and so on. A couple of them used computers when they were working but gave up using it after retirement. A couple of users never used a computer at all. The study was conducted at Delhi and Kolkata, India.

4.4.2 Material

We have used a Windows 7 HP computer with 54 cm $\times$ 33 cm monitor having 1920 $\times$ 1080 pixels resolution to record users' performance with the e-Shopping system. We used a Tobii Tx2 eye-gaze tracker to record eye-gaze. We used the same

Fig. 4.3 e-Shopping interface

algorithm described in the previous chapter to move the pointer on the screen. A standard Logitech mouse was used to record performance with mouse. We used the NASA TLX score sheet (available at Appendix 2) to measure cognitive load.

4.4.3   Procedure

The users were instructed to buy a few items using the e-Shopping interface (Fig. 4.3) using mouse and eye-gaze tracker. The mouse-based interaction did not involve target prediction system while the eye-gaze tracking based system had the target prediction on. After repeating the process a few times, they were instructed to fill up the TLX score sheet. The order of input options (mouse and eye-gaze tracker) was randomized to minimize the order effect.

The process of buying an item involved the following steps:

1. Pointing and clicking on one of the combo boxes.
2. Pointing and clicking on the button having the desired item (like camera, computer, etc., refer Fig. 4.3). On clicking a button, the interface shows a list of cameras, computers, and so on.
3. Pointing and clicking on the button having the desired product like a particular computer brand or a particular book.
4. Repeating above steps to add more items to shopping cart.
5. Pointing and clicking on 'Check Out' button at the right sides of the screen (Fig. 4.3).
6. Repeating the whole procedure (steps 1–5) two to three times using both mouse and eye-gaze tracker.

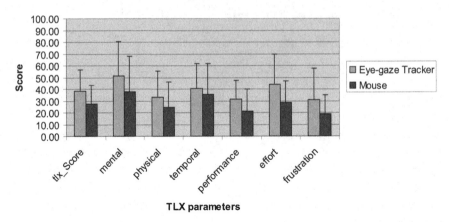

Fig. 4.4 NASA TLX score comparison between eye-gaze tracker and mouse

In case of eye-gaze tracking based system, pointing was performed by looking at the screen element and clicking was performed by pressing the spacebar of the keyboard.

4.4.4   Results

All eight users could undertake the trial and completed the task. Figure 4.4 below shows the cognitive load in terms of NASA TLX scores.

The columns correspond to average score, while the Y error bars signify standard deviation. Users scored higher TLX scores for eye-gaze tracker (mean 38.48, SD 17.85) than mouse (mean 27.66, SD 15.67) though the difference was not significant in a paired two-tailed t-test.

The button selection time was measured as the difference in time between two button selections or the time difference between selection of a combo box and next button press. The time involves pointing to the target and selecting it. The button selection time was significantly less for eye-gaze tracking based system than mouse (Figs. 4.5 and 4.6) in a Wilcoxon Signed-Rank Test ($Z=-2.84, p<0.01, r=-0.33$).

In the present experimental set up, we have defined error or wrong selection as follows:

- Users selecting same item twice consecutively.
- Users selecting 'Remove last item' button.
- Users selecting 'Clear All' button.
- We found users committed 4 wrong selections among 93 selections for eye-gaze tracking system and 1 wrong selection among 79 selections using mouse. The error rate is below 5% in both cases.

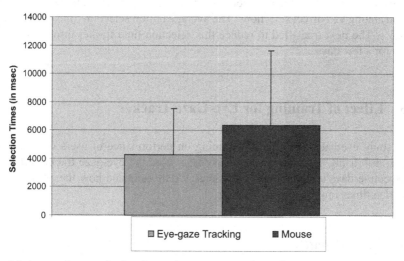

Fig. 4.5 Average button selection times using eye-gaze tracker and mouse

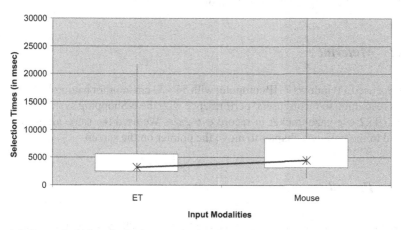

Fig. 4.6 Box and whisker plot for button selection times using eye-gaze tracker and mouse

4.4.5   *Discussion*

This study demonstrates that for an easy-to-use interface, novice users can complete tasks quicker using eye-gaze tracker than mouse, though the eye-gaze tracker tends to produce more cognitive load than mouse. It may be noted that none of these users used eye-gaze tracker before, though six of them used mouse before. In comparison to the first study, users were never stuck with the eye-gaze tracking based system and we recorded only four occasions where users took more than 10 s to select a button among 93 correct selections. The average button selection time also reduced to 4.3 s. The next trial tried to reduce this selection time further through training users for a few days.

4.5   Effect of Training for Eye-Gaze Tracker

This study evaluates the effect of training on performance of users while undertaking task using eye-gaze tracker. Two users used the eye-gaze tracker for three consecutive days undertaking six sessions. We investigated how the pointing and selection times improved with training.

4.5.1   Participants

We collected data from two users—participant 1 was a 62-year-old man, while participant 2 was a 26-year-old woman. None of them used eye-gaze tracker based system before but otherwise expert computer users and operates computers regularly. The study was conducted at Kolkata, India.

4.5.2   Material

We have used a Windows 7 HP computer with 54×33 cm monitor having 1920×1080 pixels resolution to record users' performance with the e-Shopping system. We used a Tobii Tx2 eye-gaze tracker to record eye gaze. We used the same algorithm described in the previous chapter to move the pointer on the screen.

4.5.3   Procedure

Participants were instructed to buy a few items and check out using the e-Shopping interface of Fig. 4.3. They undertook the trial twice every day for 3 consecutive days. Each session lasted from 5 to 10 min.

4.5.4   Results

We recorded 48 min 43 s of interaction from participant 1 and 54 min and 18 sec. of interaction from participant 2. We analyzed the change in button selection times across sessions for both participants and also investigated changes in selection

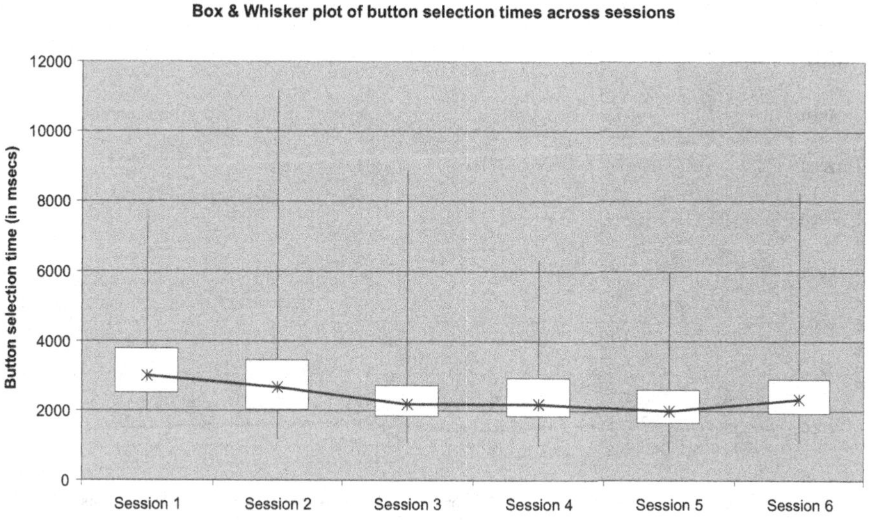

Box & Whisker plot of button selection times across sessions

Fig. 4.7 Box and whisker plot for button selection times for participant 1

times during each individual session. The median of selection times (Figs. 4.7 and 4.8) were 2.9 s and 2.8 s for participants 1 and 2 respectively, for the first session while it was reduced to less than 2 s after 4th session for participant 1 and after 2nd session for participant 2. There was a slight increase in the median selection time for participant 1 in the last session.

The average selection times also showed a decreasing trend (Figs. 4.9 and 4.10). We found a significant effect of session on selection times in one-way ANOVA (F (5, 679)=10.98, $p<0.001$ for participant 1 and F (5, 1,059)=9.75, $p<0.001$ for participant 2).

A *USER* × *SESSION* Factorial ANOVA found a significant effect of *SESSION* (F (5, 270)=10.41, $p<0.01$, $\eta^2=0.16$) but did not find a significant effect of *USER* at $p<0.05$. There was also a significant interaction effect between *USER* and *SESSION* (F (4, 216.54[1])=3.08, $p<0.05$, $\eta^2=0.05$). A multivariate test also confirmed significant effects of *SESSION* (F (5, 50)=9.1, $p<0.01$, $\eta^2=0.48$) and interaction effect of *USER* and *SESSION* (F (5, 50)=3.46, $p<0.01$, $\eta^2=0.26$). The pair-wise comparison among different sessions found

- A significant effect of session 1 with sessions 3, 4, 5, and 6 at $p<0.05$
- A significant effect of session 2 with session 5 at $p<0.5$

The pair-wise comparison did not find any other significant effect at $p<0.05$.

We also investigated the within subject contrasts and found a significant effect of linear (F (1, 54)=31.57, $p<0.01$, $\eta^2=0.37$) and quadratic (F (1, 54)=6.38, $p<0.01$, $\eta^2=0.11$) contrasts for *SESSION*.

---

[1] The *df* is fractional due to the application of Greenhouse-Geisser correction.

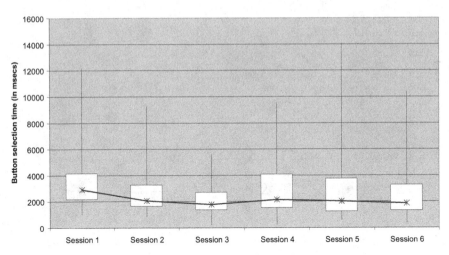

Fig. 4.8 Box and whisker plot for button selection times for participant 2

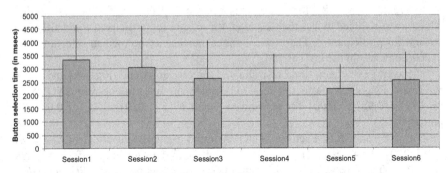

Fig. 4.9 Average for button selection times for participant 1

We have analyzed the learning effect during each individual session (Figs. 4.11 and 4.12). During first session, both participants generated a U-shaped learning curve indicating their selection time initially decreases (after approximately 100 s) and then increases again perhaps due to fatigue. For session 1, participant 2's learning curve shows this effect more prominently than participant 1. However, the learning curves turn almost horizontal after third session for participant 1 and after first session for participant 2. It indicates that participants were no longer going through a learning phase during the session. However participant 1's last session generated an increase in the selection time, perhaps due to fatigue or boredom.

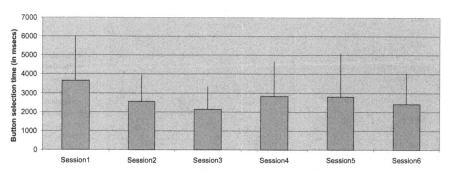

Fig. 4.10 Average for button selection times for participant 2

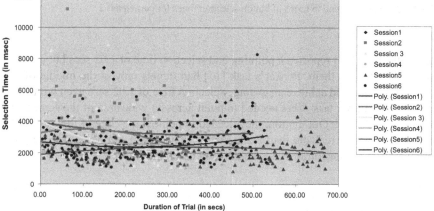

Fig. 4.11 Learning trend in terms of button selection times for participant 1

4.5.5   *Discussion*

This study demonstrates that with a simple and easy-to-use interface, users can point and select using eye-gaze tracker within 2 s. It also demonstrated that even first time users can learn to use eye-gaze tracking after going through training. The significant effect of quadratic contrast also supports the existence of a learning pattern. The pair-wise comparison shows users attained optimum speed after approximately two sessions. The individual analysis shows that the training duration differs between two participants—the elder participant took 20 min (3 sessions) before having nearly uniform selection times, while the younger participant could do it only after using the system for approximately 7 min (1 session). Although Penkar

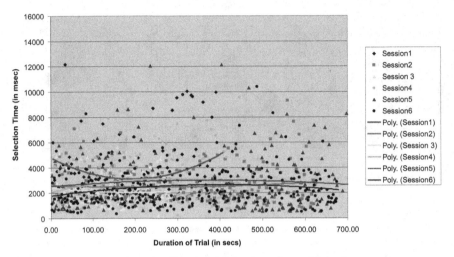

Fig. 4.12 Learning trend in terms of button selection times for participant 2

and colleagues [17] reported a pointing and selection time of 1.02 secs but our task was different than them. Penkar's task [17] had targets only at the middle of the screen so they could achieve an average selection time of 1.02 secs even with 1 sec dwell time. In our task users needed to point across a wide area of the screen and for pressing 'Check Out' button, they needed to point at the edge of the screen. So the task was more realistic than Penkar's task. This result can be used to develop training program for future eye-gaze tracking based interfaces.

4.6   Conclusion

This chapter presents a set of user trials on representative applications through eye-gaze tracking based systems. Researchers in India already investigated eye-gaze tracking based interfaces for text typing [2, 4]; however, using eye-gaze tracking for general navigation through screens and incorporation of the target prediction technology is novel. The first study uses a web browser and a Google Maps interface. It shows that even first-time users can interact with eye-gaze tracking but occasionally failed in completing the task. The second study uses an interface suitable for eye-gaze tracking and found that first-time users can point and select quicker using eye-gaze tracking than conventional mouse though at the cost of slight increase in cognitive load. The third study confirmed that selection time can further be reduced with training. Overall, this chapter aims to demonstrate that Indian users may be benefitted through novel modalities of interaction like eye-gaze tracking. However, further research is essential to develop practical eye-gaze tracking based systems.

based systems. For example, infrared-based noninvasive eye trackers (like the one we used in our studies) can often fail to track eyes for bi-focal glasses, half reading glasses, or photo-chromatic glasses, which are common for Indian middle-aged and elderly users. Future research should look at developing noninvasive eye-gaze trackers that can work in similar situations.

References

1. Vertegaal, R. (2008). *A Fitts' Law comparison of eye tracking and manual input in the selection of visual targets.* Proceedings of the International Conference of Multimodal Interaction 2008, pp. 241–248, New York, USA.
2. Gupta, A., & Balram, N. (2013). *Objective comparisions between gesture based nbsp; Exploration based touchscreen text typing keyboards.* Proceedings of 11th Asia Pacific Conference on Computer Human interaction, Bangalore, India.
3. Penkar, A. M., Lutteroth, C., & Weber G. (2012). Designing for the Eye-Design Parameters for Dwell in Gaze Interaction, OZCHI.
4. Sarcar, S., Panwar, P., & Chakraborty, T. (2013). *Eyeboard++: An enhanced eye gaze-based text entry system in Hindi.* Proceedings of 11th Asia Pacific Conference on Computer Human interaction, Bangalore, India.

Chapter 5
Concluding Remarks

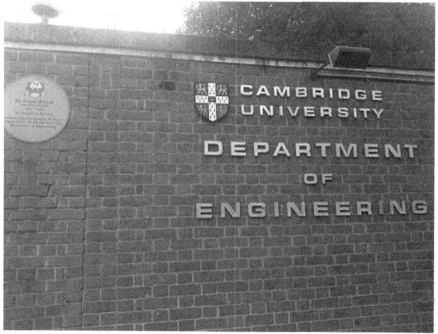

My office, the blue plaque says that the same place saw the invention of Jet engine!!

The first computer science course was the 'Diploma in Numerical Analysis and Automatic Computing', taught at University of Cambridge computer Laboratory [4] starting in 1953. In India, Indian Institute of Technology at Kanpur (IIT, Kanpur) [1] pioneered 'computer science education with the initial computer-related courses starting in August 1963 on an IBM 1620 system'. Interestingly, this 10-year gap was also present in widespread adoption of computers and related interactive technology in India. While personal computers were widespread in the late 1980s in developed

P. Biswas, *Inclusive Human Machine Interaction for India,*
Human–Computer Interaction Series, DOI 10.1007/978-3-319-06500-7_5,
© Springer International Publishing Switzerland 2014

countries, it was not until the late 1990s and early 2000s that computers become widely available to common Indian users. The result was a middle-aged and elderly generation that did not 'grow up' with computers. They can feel the benefit of computing and information technology in their work but still find existing interfaces non-intuitive or difficult to learn and remember.

The information and communication technology (ICT) related digital divide has been already investigated in detail. Keniston [2] classified digital divide into four categories comparing the Indian context with USA and summarized ten lessons for successfully disseminating benefit of ICT in India. Smith and Dunckley [3] emphasized the need of correct cultural model to improve interaction experience of users in developing countries. Walton, Marsden and Vukovic [5] investigated cultural difference in more detail for South African students and pointed out key differences in interpreting hierarchical structures among native students.

In India, research on human–computer interaction made significant contribution on developing multi-lingual systems for Indian languages. However, there is not much research on investigating issues with existing electronic devices and exploring possibilities of using state-of-the-art interactive devices for common computing tasks.

This book targets the middle-aged and elderly population of India across a wide geographical area and professions. It presents a case study of

- Generating user requirements
- Modifying existing systems to facilitate man–machine interaction
- Developing new interaction techniques
- Designing new interfaces for representative application like shopping, banking, agriculture and so on.

The book does not aim to be a replacement for a standard textbook on interaction design or human–computer interaction; rather it reports a series of user trials, new technologies and literature survey to supplement existing theories and guidelines. Results from the user trials can be used by professionals to develop new eye-gaze or head-movement tracking systems and related applications. The web-based user model can be used to personalize existing e-governance applications. Finally, the book can also be used to teach students, interaction designers and early stage researchers about designing user interfaces, user surveys and user trials.

References

1. IIT Kanpur. Department of Computer Science and Engineering. (2014) http://www.cse.iitk. ac.in. Accessed 13 Feb 2014.
2. Keniston, K., & Kumar, D. (Eds.). (2003) *The four digital divides.* Delhi: Sage.
3. Smith, A., & Dunckley, L. (2007) Issues for human–computer interaction in developing countries, CHI 2007.
4. University of Cambridge. Computer Laboratory, Faculty of Computer Science and Technology. (2014) http://www.cl.cam.ac.uk. Accessed 13 Feb 2014.
5. Walton, M., Marsden, G., & Vukovic, V. (2001) "Visual literacy" as challenge to the internationalization of interfaces: A study of South African student web users, CHI-SA 2001.

Appendix

1. Sample of consent form
2. NASA TLX score sheet
3. User profile format
4. Rules to personalize interfaces

-

P. Biswas, *Inclusive Human Machine Interaction for India,*
Human–Computer Interaction Series, DOI 10.1007/978-3-319-06500-7,
© Springer International Publishing Switzerland 2014

Consent Form

Research Consent Form

This consent form, a copy of which has been given to you, is only part of the process of informed consent. It should give you the basic idea of what the research is about and what your participation will involve. If you would like more detail about something not mentioned here, or information not included here, please ask. Please take the time to read this form carefully and to understand any accompanying information.

● **Research Project Title**

IUATC – India UK Advanced Technology Centre of Excellence

● **Purpose of the Study**

The study aims to evaluate an eye-gaze tracking based electronic shopping application.

● **Participant Recruitment and Selection**

Anyone more than 60 years old and having basic knowledge of operating computers can participate.

● **Procedure**

The study involves interacting with an electronic shopping application using an eye-gaze tracker. The participants need to mimic the process of buying some electronic items and books by pressing a few buttons in a computer screen. The study will not ask for any credit card or banking details.

● **Data Collection**

Data will be stored electronically.

● **Confidentiality**

Confidentiality and participant anonymity will be strictly maintained. All information gathered will be used for statistical analysis only and no names or other identifying characteristics will be stated in the final or any other reports. All data will be identified only by a code (with names kept in a locked file), and will not be used or made available for any purposes other than the research project.

● **Likelihood of Discomfort**

There is no likelihood of discomfort or risk associated with participation. However, the participant can leave the experiment at any point of time if he feels fatigue or loses interest.

● **Researcher**

Dr. Pradipta Biswas is a researcher at the University of Cambridge Engineering Design Centre. Pradipta can be contacted in the Department of Engineering at the University of Cambridge, UK. His email address is pb400@cam.ac.uk.

● **Finding out about Results**

Results will be presented at conferences and written up in journals. Results will normally be presented in terms of groups of individuals. If any individual data are presented, the data would be totally anonymous, without any means of identifying the individuals involved. The participants can find out the results of the study by contacting the researcher after July 1, 2014.

● **Agreement**

Your signature on this form indicates that you have understood to your satisfaction the information regarding participation in the research project, agree to participate as a participant and received INR 200 as reimbursement. In no way does this waive you legal rights nor release the investigators, sponsors, or involved institutions from their legal and professional responsibilities. You are free to not answer specific items or questions in interviews or on questionnaires. You are free to withdraw from the study at any time without penalty. Your continued participation should be as informed as your initial consent, so you should feel free to ask for clarification or new information throughout your participation. If you have further questions concerning matters related to this research, please contact the researcher.

_____   _____

Participant   **Date**

NASA TLX Form

User Profile Format

Mandatory for Adapting Interface

Variable name	Description	Data Type
Username	A unique id of user	String
Password	Log In credential	String
Age	Age of user in years	Integer
Sex	Sex of user	Integer
Height	Standing height of user	Integer
Volume	Preferred volume of speakers	Double
fontSize	Minimum font size of interface captions	Integer
fontColour	Preferred fore colour of buttons	String
cursorSize	Size of cursor	Double
cursorColour	Colour of cursor	String
Colour blindness	Presence and type of colour blindness, used to predict colour contrast of interface	Integer
Tremor	Presence of Tremor or Spasm in hand	Integer

Optional Parameters for Advanced User Modelling

Variable name	Description	Data type
Username	A unique id of user	String
Password	Log In credential	String
Age	Age of user in years	Integer
Sex	Sex of user	Integer
Height	Standing height of user	Integer
Volume	Preferred volume of speakers	Double
fontSize	Minimum font size of interface captions	Integer
fontColour	Preferred fore colour of buttons	String
cursorSize	Size of cursor	Double
cursorColour	Colour of cursor	String
Visual acuity	Visual acuity of user, used to predict minimum font size	Acuity
Contrast sensitivity	Contrast sensitivity of user, used to predict minimum font size	Integer
Scotoma	Number of scotoma in visual field, used to predict minimum font size and appropriate modality of interaction	Integer
FieldLossP	Amount of peripheral visual field, used to predict minimum font size and appropriate modality of interaction	Integer
FieldLossC	Amount of central visual field, used to predict minimum font size and appropriate modality of interaction	Integer
Colour blindness	Presence and type of colour blindness, used to predict colour contrast of interface	Integer
Macular degeneration	Presence of macular degeneration, used to predict minimum font size and appropriate modality of interaction	Integer
halfK	Minimum hearing level in dB at 500 Hz	Integer
oneK	Minimum hearing level in dB at 1 kHz	Integer
twoK	Minimum hearing level in dB at 2 kHz	Integer
fourK	Minimum hearing level in dB at 4 kHz	Integer
eightK	Minimum hearing level in dB at 8 kHz	Integer
TMT	Time taken to complete Trail Making Test	Integer
DIGSYM	Score in Digit Symbol Test	Integer
Grip strength	Maximum grip strength of dominant hand	Integer
Tremor	Presence of tremor or spasm in hand	Integer
ROMW	Active range of motion of wrist	Double

Rules to Personalize Interfaces

Fontsize

At Server:

```
visualAngle = (FontSize in pixel / ScreenY) * (ScreenLength /
dist2Screen)
```

At Client:

```
FontSize in pixel == ScreenY * visualAngle * (dist2Screen
/ScreenLength)
```

Colour Contrast

If the colour blindness is Protanopia or Deuteranopia (Red-Green) it recommends

White foreground colour in Blue background

For any other type of colour blindness it recommends

White foreground in Black background or vice versa

Line Spacing

```
If tremor is positive
    //Line spacing will be double to normal
    lineSpacing=2.0
Else
//Calculate Grip Strength
      If sex = male then
          GripStrength = 26.85 - 0.36 * age + 0.15 * height
      Else
          GripStrength = 22.01 - 0.36 * age + 0.15 * height
      End if

      If GripStrength < =10 then
          //Line spacing will be double to normal
          lineSpacing = 2.0
      Else If GripStrength < =20 then
          //Line spacing will be 1.5times to normal
          lineSpacing = 1.5
      Else
          //Line Spacing will not change
          lineSpacing = 1.0
      End If
End If
```

Button Spacing

If users have tremor, less than 10 kg of Grip strength or 80° of ROM in wrist

Minimum button spacing = 0.2 *distance of target from centre of screen

If users have less than 25 kg of Grip strength

Minimum button spacing = 0.15 *distance of target from centre of screen

  else

Minimum button spacing = 0.05 * length of diagonal of the screen

Modality

If User has Maccular Degeneration or User is Blind
                BestIP = "Voice"
                If DeviceType = TV"
                    BestOP = "AudioCaption"
                Else

                    BestOP = "ScreenReader"
                End If

  ElseIf GRIP STRENGTH < 10Kg Or tremor is positive Then
'Severe Motor Impairment with vision
                Select Case DeviceType
                    Case 'Mobile'
                        BestIP = "BigButton"
                    Case 'Laptop'
                        BestIP = "TrackBall or Scanning"
                    Case 'Tablet'
                        BestIP = "Stylus"
                    Case 'PC'
                        BestIP = "TrackBall or Scanning"
                    Case 'TV'
                        BestIP = "SecondScreenBigButton"
                End Select

                BestOP = "Screen"

```
    ElseIf GRIP STRENGTH < 20Kg Then 'Moderate Motor Impairment
with vision
                 Select Case DeviceType
                        Case 'Mobile'
                              BestIP = "BigButton"
                        Case 'Laptop'
                              BestIP = "TrackBall or Mouse"
                        Case 'Tablet'
                              BestIP = "Stylus"
                        Case 'PC'
                              BestIP = "TrackBall or Mouse"
                        Case 'TV'
                              BestIP = "SecondScreenBigButton"
                 End Select

                 BestOP = "Screen"


    ElseIf ACTIVE RANGE OF MOTION OF WRIST < 100° Then

                 Select Case DeviceType
                        Case 'Mobile'
                              BestIP = "Stylus or BigButton"
                        Case 'Laptop'
                              BestIP = "Trackball or Mouse"
                        Case 'Tablet'

                              BestIP = "Stylus"
                        Case 'PC'
                              BestIP = "Trackball or Mouse"
                        Case 'TV'
                              BestIP = "BasicRemote"
                 End Select

                 BestOP = "Screen"

    Else 'User without visual or motor impairment

                 BestIP = "DirectManipulation"
                 BestOP = "Screen"
             End If
```

Index

P. Biswas, *Inclusive Human Machine Interaction for India,*
Human–Computer Interaction Series, DOI 10.1007/978-3-319-06500-7,
© Springer International Publishing Switzerland 2014

Printed in the United States
By Bookmasters